SUTTON VENY

A History

by

THE SUTTON VENY HISTORY GROUP

PHILIP CLARK KATE COLLIER DAVID EYRES BARBARA HUNT
STEPHEN OXLADE JILL RUSSELL

with chapters from
STELLA MADDOCK AND SALLY THOMSON

First published in the United Kingdom in 2017

for The Sutton Veny History Group

by The Hobnob Press, 30c Deverill Road Trading Estate, Sutton Veny, Warminster BA12 7BZ
www.hobnobpress.co.uk

British Library Cataloguing in Publication Data
A catalogue record for this book is available from the British Library

ISBN 978-1-906978-48-8

Typeset in Adobe Garamond Pro 11/14 pt. Typesetting and origination by John Chandler.

Printed by Lightning Source

CONTENTS

ACKNOWLEDGEMENTS AND THANKS

At least 70 individuals and businesses helped us with the research and production of this book. Our requests for information and assistance have been met with amazing enthusiasm. People have been delighted to give us facts and figures, stories and photographs; several have given us access to family papers, memoirs and memorabilia. Several firms gave resource and staff time for a nominal fee or sometimes at no charge (one for instance waived their costs but when pressed, asked merely a contribution towards the staff biscuit tin).

It is inevitable that if we sought to name everybody, there would be accidental omissions. So, it is with considerable reluctance that we have decided that we would not specifically mention any individual or organisation.

Where we think it necessary, we have sought copyright holder's permission to use their material. To these we say thank you. But if by chance we have overlooked someone, then we apologise.

The costs of research, materials, art-work and printing have amounted to a tidy sum and, but for generous financial support from the following, this publication would simply not have been possible:

Chalke Valley History Trust
Cranborne Chase AONB Sustainable Development Fund
Longbridge Deverill History Group
Private donors
Ray Thomas, Property Services Ltd, Warminster
Roy Vallis, Harrison Vallis Gilbert Ltd, Upton-Upon-Severn, Worcs
Sutton Veny Parish Council
Wylye Dentistry, Warminster

To these and everyone who have so freely given us backing, we say on behalf of ourselves and the present and future residents of Sutton Veny parish, thank you; thank you very much indeed.

INTRODUCTION

A S FOLK TRAVEL the Wylye Valley road winding its way from Salisbury to Warminster, few have the impulse to stop at Sutton Veny; it is after all as unremarkable as the thousands of similarly unremarkable villages across the kingdom. But to those privileged to call it home, there are curiosities to be discovered.

Over the years there have been several booklets, pamphlets and publications about individual features of the village, but there is no overall account of its past: why did the original settlement come to take root where it did? Why not for instance, a mile or so further north or south, or east or west? Was there a specific reason or was it simply by chance?

The History Group was originally formed to research and assemble historical information about the parish community. As this progressed, it soon became clear that there was so much material that it could not be included in a single volume. This book therefore looks at the development and relationship between the parish geography, its population, infrastructure and institutions. The reader has been identified as the person sitting on the Beeline bus, travelling along the winding valley road from Salisbury to Warminster. Memories about village organisations, people and events which formed the very *essence* of the original community, are being gathered and recorded for publication later.

The material was researched and written by villagers. However when it came to Ancient and Early history, the team was stumped. Stella Maddock (an archaeologist) and Sally Thompson (a historian), who are not villagers, were able to step in and write those chapters.

This book is a non-profit community venture. The costs of research, the artwork and printing have amounted to tidy sum which was self-funded until grants, donations and sponsorships materialised to help alleviate a shortfall. It is anticipated that the remaining shortfall will be recouped from sales. After that, any 'profit' will be donated to parish charities, clubs and organisations until book supplies are exhausted.

In thinking about the parish, we imagine that it epitomises Rural England. In October 1953, the Wiltshire News printed a whole page about Sutton Veny which included the following passage:

...I had a look in on the Sutton Veny-Deverill Road blacksmith, Norman Cooper at the Forge. As of old, the usual gossip was going on with 'Varmer' Coward holding forth in the manner of the rural philosopher type he is. He said as he squatted on a low bench with his cap at a jaunty angle: 'we've got too many importees in Sutton Veny. There's nothing wrong with the place itself. We be a happy contented lot out yer, and don't want any outsiders telling us what they think is vor our good.'

It is not *quite* like that any more

PROLOGUE

IT IS DAWN. You have climbed onto a substantial pile of earth to get a better view of your surroundings. There is no date, but in due course, it will be loosely described as 4,000 years before the birth of Christ – the Neolithic Period.

As the sun rises, you can make out that you are in a wooded valley with marshy ground to the north. You can see that to the south, the land rises steeply to distant downs. At the foot of the mound there is a path crossing in front of you and, beyond that, more marshy ground fed from a stream.

You can hear chanting and, looking eastwards, you see a procession coming in your direction. It has come from some kind of meeting place and they are carrying something, a body; this is a funeral procession.

It will make its way through the stream and over the track to where you are standing – because you are on the top of what we call a Long Barrow.

One day the track will have a name – Duck Street. The stream rises from ground several hundred yards away to the south at Springhead. On the mound from where the procession began, will one day stand a church – St Leonard's, Sutton Veny.

Fantasy perhaps. But then, is it?

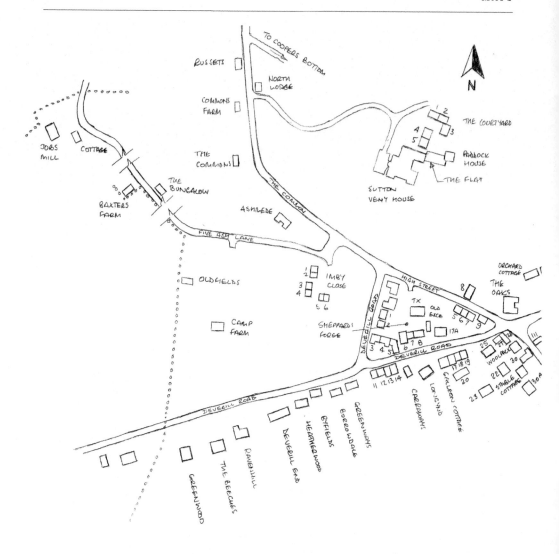

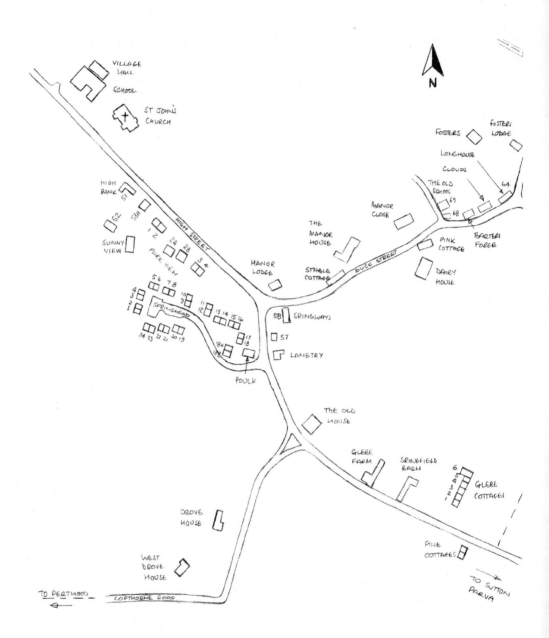

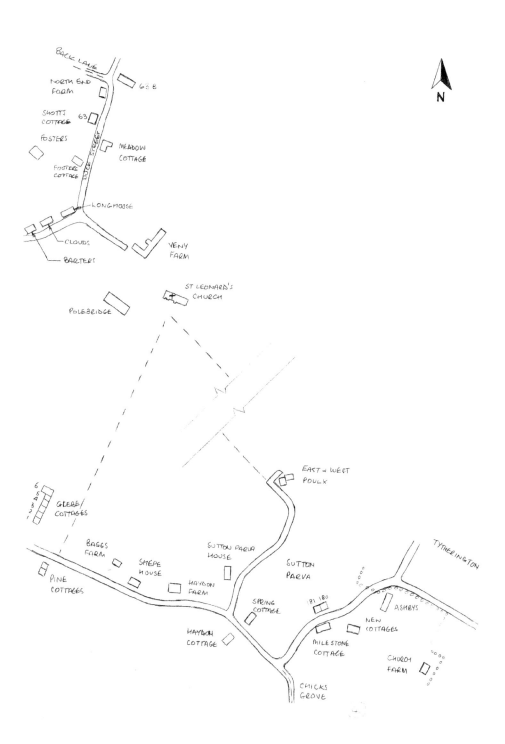

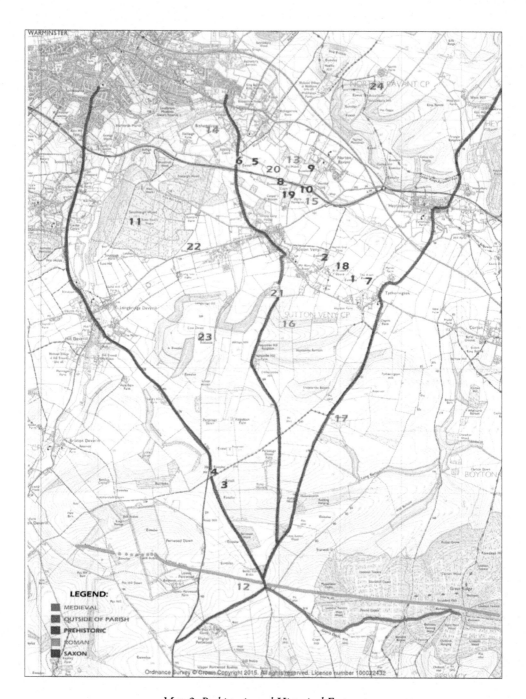

Map 2: Prehistoric and Historical Features

I
EARLY HISTORY

PREHISTORY
by Stella Maddock

Sutton Veny in prehistory – the time before the Romans arrived

L IKE ALL THE PARISHES along the Wylye Valley, Sutton Veny has a landscape rich with the remains and traces of prehistoric human activity. Some of these remains are clearly visible, some less so, whilst some can now only be seen as cropmarks in the soil revealed on aerial photos and Google Earth. Much has been lost through ploughing and gradual erosion but, although often damaged, many features have survived to this day.

There is evidence of people living in the Sutton Veny area for at least the last 5,500 years. Although the following is a description of what was happening in prehistoric times and concentrates on the area within the 21st century parish of Sutton Veny, it is important to recognise that the current parish boundary reflects much later communities and not those that existed in prehistory; the prehistoric features within modern Sutton Veny parish cannot be seen in isolation from others in neighbouring parishes and the Wylye Valley as a whole.

Sutton Veny in the Neolithic (New Stone Age) period, c.4000 – c.2500 BC

I T WAS IN THE Neolithic period that people in Britain started to manage woodland, plant crops and domesticate animals. From around 3750 BC they built long barrows – communal tombs holding the remains of their dead. These would have been conspicuous monuments in the landscape and many are still visible today. The West Kennet Long Barrow near Avebury at 100m long is a fine example and well worth a visit as it is possible to walk inside the now empty burial chambers.

Along the Wylye Valley, there are several known and visible long barrows sited on the valley floor – Sherrington, Corton, and King Barrow Bishopstrow – as well as others higher up on ridges above the valley. In Sutton Veny, the mound visible east of St Leonard's church on the north side of the footpath to Tytherington (No.1 on map 2) is probably the remains of a long barrow. It has suffered some damage and been cut by a track so it is now less clear whether it is a long barrow or a later round barrow. However, it fits well into the sequence of long barrows sited in the Wylye Valley.

Probable long barrow east of St Leonard's Church

There is another barrow in Sutton Veny that has also been considered to be a long barrow. It is in a field on the west side of Duck Street (No. 2 on Map 2). It too has been damaged and, like the one east of the old church, it has never been excavated, so exactly what it is and when it was constructed is uncertain.

Possible long barrow west side of Duck Street

Later in the Neolithic period, other large monuments such as earth henges and stone circles were constructed. The first phase of Stonehenge, – the outer bank, ditch, and inner bank – was started about 3000 BC. At Sutton Common, in a field on the north side of the Longbridge Deverill road (OS Grid Reference ST 885419), and just visible, is a circular bank with a segmented internal ditch (No. 22). This may be a Neolithic henge, about 80m in diameter, one of only about 18 known henges in Wiltshire.

Sutton Veny in the Copper Age, c.2500 – c.2000 BC, and the Bronze Age, c.2000 – c.800 BC

A T THE START OF this period some significant monuments were built both here and abroad - in Egypt, the Pyramids of Giza and the Sphinx, and in Wiltshire, the great sarsen trilithons at Stonehenge and the Silbury Hill mound near Avebury.

Trade routes were opening up and it is probable that the Wylye Valley would have been an important route for the growing trade in raw materials such as copper and tin to make bronze and for the export of surplus grain. The Sutton Veny area also lay along the line of several other important communication and trade routes that may have had their origins in the Neolithic period. The prehistoric routeway known as The Ridgeway that runs from East Anglia to Devon following the chalk ridges made its way across Salisbury Plain on a variety of routes. Depending on which route it had taken, it crossed the River Wylye at Boreham, Heytesbury, or Longbridge Deverill before heading for Dorset. The broad lines of these routeways are illustrated on map 2.

The Boreham route south of the Wylye follows approximately the line of the modern road to Bishopstrow and Sutton Veny where it heads south from the High Street and up Hill Road (sometimes called Chalk Path) along the road leading over Whiten Hill to Haycombe Hill Farm (ST895401). The Heytesbury route follows approximately the line of the modern road to Tytherington, then south up the west side of Tytherington Hill along the track that is now the Sutton Veny parish boundary (ST 914401). The Longbridge Deverill route goes up Lords Hill to Parsonage Down and then along the track past Pertwood Wood (ST893373).

All three routes more or less converge at the southernmost point of Sutton Veny parish (ST898366) before heading towards Pertwood and East Knoyle. At the convergence they are crossed by yet another important routeway – the Groveley ridgeway – which runs east west along Great Ridge and the watershed between the Wylye and the Nadder valleys. It was once part of a throughway that began at the Kent coast and came eventually to the Mendips and the Bristol Channel. The Groveley ridgeway was later used by the Romans who developed it into a road to get to the lead mines in the Mendips.

Also at this time, there was a change in Britain in the way people buried their dead. Instead of the earlier communal long barrows, round barrows, each containing the cremated or buried remains of one or more people, were constructed. The people buried in these mounds were often buried with precious objects including gold and bronze items suggesting their wealth and importance.

In the area, there are a great many of these round barrows – within Sutton Veny parish alone there may have been as many as 32. Some are still obvious features in the landscape (Nos. 3,4,5,6,7,8,9) including in particular, The Knoll (No. 7) in the field north of the path from St Leonard's church to Tytherington. Many more have disappeared but can be detected from circular crop or soil marks that delineate the ditch around the mound, visible on aerial photos and Google Earth. A large number of these barrows, possibly as many as 19, are sited on the valley floor including a no longer visible group of at least seven in the fields north-east of St Leonard's church, forming what is known as a barrow cemetery. It seems that the low-lying, possibly even waterlogged, land close to the river was particularly used for these burial mounds (we don't know why this was). They were being constructed around the same time as Tutankhamen was being buried in the Valley of the Kings in Egypt.

'The Knoll' – a Bronze Age round barrow east of St Leonard's church

This Google Earth image (opposite, top) shows how earthworks invisible on the ground show up as cropmarks from the air. These are in a field north of the village.

A few of the barrows in the Sutton Veny area have been excavated. One, up on the downs, was excavated in 1810 by Sir Richard Colt Hoare, the owner of Stourhead, and William Cunnington of Heytesbury. They found a cremation with some perforated bone buttons, a bronze awl and segmented tin beads. The buttons and the awl are at the Wiltshire Museum in Devizes. Now destroyed, this barrow (roughly near ST890390) was of a rare type of round barrow known as a disc barrow. Two barrows near Pit Meads (No. 9 and one no longer visible) were excavated in 1786/87 by Mrs Catherine Downes. Both contained cremations, one within an urn.

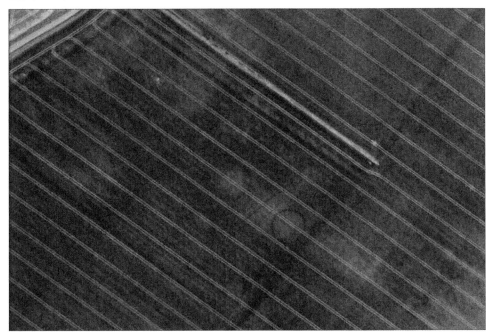

Earthworks invisible from ground level

left: Bone buttons from the disc barrow on the downs excavated in 1810.
right: Bronze awl from the disc barrow on the downs excavated in 1810.
Photos © Wiltshire Museum, Devizes

A very interesting barrow at ST913415, west of The Knoll barrow, and possibly part of the barrow cemetery mentioned above, was excavated in 1964 as it was fast disappearing. It was of a type known as a bell barrow. In the centre of the mound was the skeleton of a man in a planked wooden coffin, together with a clay food vessel, a small cup and a bronze dagger. On the edge of the mound was an urn containing the cremated remains of an adult, probably a woman. A further burial was found on the edge of the mound. This was a man with a sword cut to the head and is probably a much later Anglo-Saxon intrusive burial. The grave goods from the coffin burial, as well as the cremation urn, are in Salisbury Museum. The barrow however, is no longer visible on the ground.

left: Pygmy cup from the bell barrow west of The Knoll excavated in 1964.
right: Food vessel from the bell barrow west of The Knoll excavated in 1964.
Photos © The Salisbury Museum

In 1987, excavations by Wessex Archaeology in advance of works related to the construction of the Warminster bypass at Mootlebury/Moot Hill (ST 905427) revealed an Early Bronze Age round barrow (No. 10) containing a 'high-status' burial of a male with a copper alloy knife, bone belt hook, whetstone, bone needle and a miniature pottery vessel. These items can be seen on display in the Wessex Gallery at Salisbury Museum.

In the middle of the Bronze Age, an increase in population led to more organised farming and fields were created delineated by ditches. The traces of these field systems can still be seen on the downs above the Wylye Valley, for example on Wylye Down, and many more are visible on aerial photos. There are several field systems on the downs above Sutton Veny (e.g. at ST890388) which may date back to the Bronze Age and which continued into the Iron Age.

Later in the Bronze Age a huge system of boundary ditches was built across much of southern England. These 'linear ditches' appear to have divided the land into blocks, each block containing a portion of each type of land – e.g. valley floor, slope, down. Each block might have represented the land holding of a particular kin group or community and contain a dozen or so farmsteads. Grim's Ditch which runs along the ridge that forms the watershed between the Wylye and the Nadder is very likely to be one of these Late Bronze Age/Early Iron Age linear ditches and part of a system of land division related to farming. It is still visible today along most of its length, (e.g. at ST899364), and it forms the southern boundary of many of today's Wylye Valley parishes.

Whereabouts in Sutton Veny parish the people who farmed these fields and buried their elite dead in round burial mounds lived, has not yet been discovered. But it seems

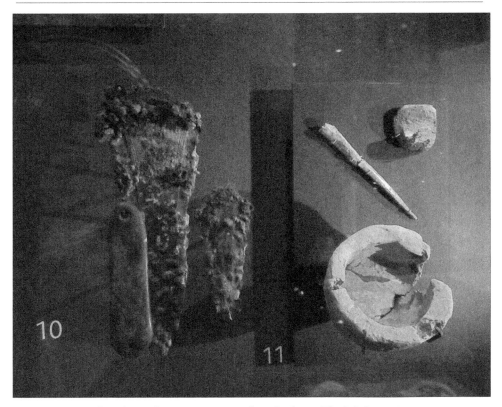

Artefacts from a barrow at Moot Hill on display at The Salisbury Museum
Photo © Salisbury Museum

safe to assume that there was at least one Bronze Age settlement in the Sutton Veny area. Two pits containing Bronze Age pottery found near the bridleway that runs from the A350 north-east across Parsonage Down (ST895385) may be a clue, but settlement may also have been in the valley, now hidden under much later dwellings. Flint tools were found during work ahead of road improvements on the A350 at Lords Hill (ST889389) not far from the pits and the field systems. There was certainly an important Late Bronze Age/Early Iron Age settlement adjacent to the Sutton Veny parish boundary on Cow Down (ST887405) in Longbridge Deverill parish (No. 23), which must have been a focus for a large area around including Sutton Veny. It included a very large round structure that might indicate the presence of a 'chief'/leader and/or ritual activity.

Sutton Veny in the Iron Age, approx 800 BC – AD 43

IT WAS DURING this period, the indigenous people appear to have been loosely divided into groups (tribes is too categorical a word), which each held large tracts of land. The boundaries between these groups are contentious issues today; and while many think that the River Wylye was such a boundary, it was also a vital communications link and unlikely to have been a dividing line.

The people of the Sutton Veny area were almost certainly part of a group known as the *Durotriges*, whose territory comprised the whole of Dorset and the bordering edges of Wiltshire, Hampshire, Somerset, and Devon.

In the Late Bronze Age/Early Iron Age massive earthworks encircling large areas of land on hilltops were constructed, often at the junctions of the linear ditches mentioned above. These hilltop enclosures, now termed hillforts, were not necessarily built primarily for defence. They seem to have been related to the coming together of various groups of people by creating a communal focus for regular gatherings and activities including trade, social exchange, and ritual.

The earliest phase of Scratchbury hillfort (centred at ST912443) which dominates the Sutton Veny, Norton Bavant and Heytesbury areas, was built in the early Iron Age (No. 24). It lies outside the modern Sutton Veny parish boundary but it must have been used by people living in the vicinity of Sutton Veny in the Iron Age and been a very significant feature in the landscape. Later in the Iron Age many circular structures – probably roundhouses – were built inside the enclosed area of the hillfort.

Iron Age field system Pertwood Down

As well as the Late Bronze Age/Early Iron Age Cow Down settlement mentioned above, there are two other known Iron Age settlement sites in or very close to Sutton Veny parish, both with associated field systems. One is south of Tytherington Hill (No. 17). It was first investigated by Colt Hoare in 1821 and he found evidence of some 10 hut sites with field enclosures and low banks. In more recent investigations, particularly using aerial photographs, further evidence of huts has shown up to the west of this site, so that it now straddles both the modern parishes of Sutton Veny and of Heytesbury. 'Lumps and bumps' can be seen at the site and an Iron Age coin of the Durotrigian group was found close by. (See also the Roman section). The other possible settlement site is suggested by a complex of pits and a field system just to the east of the footpath that runs from North End Farm at the end of Duck Street northwards to the A36 (ST912423).

So people seem to have been living in a variety of locations in Sutton Veny in the Iron Age. The landscape would have been a patchwork of extended farms with unenclosed groups of huts and small rectangular shaped fields now known as 'Celtic fields'. These fields are still visible on aerial photos, especially those on the downs.

One other probably Iron Age feature in Sutton Veny parish is worth mentioning. This is a rectangular low earthwork enclosure in Southleigh Wood, now known as Robin Hood's Bower, (No. 11). Its purpose however, is unknown.

There are many other probable prehistoric features in Sutton Veny parish such as enclosures, pits, and ditches that can be seen on aerial photos but cannot be dated without excavation. These and all the other features discussed above, clearly suggest that Sutton Veny was quite a busy area from the Neolithic through to the coming of the Romans in AD 43, and in the Bronze Age, it had some wealthy residents!

ROMAN PERIOD (AD 46 – 450)
By Sally Thomson

BY AD55 the Romans had occupied most of the south west. In Wiltshire, the remains of several Roman towns are known, but some have been reduced to marks in the fields, only picked up by aerial photography. The remains of smaller settlements are more common, simply because more of them have survived centuries of ploughing, being situated on the downs and higher lands of the county. The Romans also built a number of roads linking their major settlements. At least six of these pass within the boundaries of

Roman coin from Pit Meads. Gallienus antoninianus (253-268 AD).
©Warminster Museum

Wiltshire and one (No. 12) was constructed just after the Conquest and runs from Old Sarum westwards, along Great Ridge to Charterhouse on Mendip. This was an important road, built to transport lead from the mines there. This road passes just south of the parish's southernmost tip.

The influence of the Roman way of life certainly made itself felt on the indigenous population, as can be seen in the remains of sophisticated buildings, pottery, imports, coinage and a commercial way of life experienced by many of the population. Rural villas and urban settlements would have required a large supporting population to supply the needs of the wealthy and the entrepreneurs of the time. And it is likely that there was considerable intermarriage between the Romans and the local population.

So far, Sutton Veny itself has very little to show for the Roman period, but no doubt in time, as search techniques are refined, more will be discovered. In the meantime, and as a result of the change of parish boundaries in 1884, land that once marked the division between Warminster, Bishopstrow, Heytesbury and Norton Bavant, was brought into Sutton Veny and with it, the parish acquired a significant Roman site. In the field known as Pit Meads, hidden beneath the earth, lie the remains of one large, or two, successive Roman villas (No. 13). The site lies surprisingly close to the Wylye and would possibly have been subject to flooding at times, perhaps leading to the eventual abandonment of the buildings. Being so close to water though, had its advantages, when trade relied heavily upon water transport and most goods destined for the villa(s) would have come up the Wylye from the Hampshire Avon. The Roman archaeology specialist, Dr Mark Corney, is fairly sure that the two Romano-British settlements on

Model of possible layout of Pit Meads Roman Villa
(By kind permission of Warminster Museum)

Knook Down, some 6k away to the east and on the north side of the Wylye, were the two 'working farms' for the villa(s) at Pit Meads, producing all the necessary grain and fodder for the community (or communities) there. The river Wylye would also of course, have provided the essential source of water.

The Pit Meads site was first discovered in 1786, when several fine tessellated pavements were found, and which subsequently have disappeared. One piece, depicting a hare, was removed to Longleat and preserved there for a time, but its whereabouts is not now known. In 1800, William Cunnington from Heytesbury excavated the site and uncovered several rooms; he recorded the dimensions of one building as being about 360ft x 90ft, the east front having a projection. The site was reopened by Richard Colt Hoare in 1820 and he wrote about his work in his celebrated volumes on *Ancient Wiltshire*. In the past it was often called the Warminster, or Norton Bavant Villa. Warminster Public Library has an excellent model of the villa(s) on display, together with some of the artefacts found there.

These are an example of fine Samian ware fragments from Pit Meads, indicative of high status Roman sites.

Fine Samian ware, from Pit Meads (By kind permission of Warminster Museum)

With a well-established villa site in the valley, it would be natural to have a place of worship nearby and it is believed that there *may* be a Roman temple site on Cotley Hill, which falls just outside the parish boundary, north of Heytesbury, but which in Roman times would have had influence over a large area of the valley, including Sutton Veny.

Again, bearing in mind that parish boundaries as such did not exist before Saxon times, just outside the parish boundary to the north-west and in Bishopstrow parish is a large earthwork of some 56 acres, called The Bury (No. 14). This was excavated by Colt Hoare and was found to contain a great depth of black soil and quantities of Roman pottery; in 1792, a huge hoard of some 30,000 bronze coins had been found in the vicinity of The Bury. There is some uncertainty about the origins of this earthwork, some believing it may have had Iron Age origins, though no remains of that era have been found. It is more likely to have been a settlement of Romano-British date, or perhaps an *oppidum,* an adaptation of a hillfort to a valley site. On the evidence found so far, The Bury shows signs of occupation from the 1st to the 4th centuries AD, covering about three quarters of the time the Romans were in Britain. It has been found to have numerous internal boundaries and there may have been official buildings on the site for the purpose of governance; thus the site would have had influence over any settlements in the area.

When the Warminster bypass was constructed in 1987, a borrow pit was opened alongside the road, to provide chalk fill. This was dug out of Mootlebury Hill (or Moot Hill) in Sutton Veny (No. 15). At the time, an investigation was undertaken by Wessex Trust for Archaeology and as well as a Bronze Age burial, (see the section on Prehistory), ditches, pits and gullies from the late Iron Age/early Romano-British period were also found, a period covering the 1st century BC to the 1st century AD.

When it came to farming in the Roman period, most fields were small and usually rectangular, managed by individual families on a small scale. When the supply of land was short, the hillsides could be utilised by ploughing flat strips along the contours of

Strip lynchets on the east side of Hill Road, Sutton Veny

the hillsides. These early lynchets, as they were known, were never very long and always in a compact unit. There are lynchets of this sort in the hillside on the east of Hill Road in Sutton Veny, which are believed to be either of Iron Age origin or Romano-British (No. 16). They could of course have been created in the earlier period and been taken over and reworked later.

On the downs above Sutton Veny, but right on the border with Heytesbury parish lie the remains of an Iron Age or Romano-British settlement (ST908391). It was first investigated by Colt Hoare in 1821 and he found evidence of some ten hut sites with field enclosures and low banks. In more recent investigations, particularly in aerial photographs, further evidence of huts has shown up to the west of this site, so that it now straddles both the modern parishes of Sutton Veny and of Heytesbury (No. 17 – see also the Iron Age section). To the south of the settlement site is evidence of a field system, almost certainly worked by the people living in the settlement. There may have been a community here for centuries and it must have proved a productive site, since it seems to have continued into the Romano-British era. Among the artefacts recovered were many iron fragments, nails, pottery, a corn-drying kiln and a T-shaped hypocaust (an under-floor Roman heating system). So even if this settlement had begun in the Iron Age, it certainly seems to have continued into the time of the Roman occupation.

SAXON PERIOD (AD 450 – AD 1066)
By Sally Thomson

AFTER THE ROMANS left Britain, there followed a long period of decline and a re-discovery of itself for the country. To this day, arguments continue over whether or not the Anglo-Saxon takeover was sudden and violent, or whether it was a gradual and fairly peaceful process; or, indeed, a mixture of the two. There is also the vexed question about continuity: whether the estates set up in Roman times continued to be run by the indigenous population, or whether even these broke down. Certainly many crafts and skills were lost and it took many centuries for some of these to be rediscovered. But when the Anglo-Saxons finally made their way into the Wylye Valley and settled in the many communities along its length, which persist, even today, they gave their own names to these settlements.

In view of the nearby Neolithic long barrow and the many Bronze Age barrows in the area, there is likely to have been a settlement in the vicinity for thousands of years, though it is not known exactly where such a settlement may have been sited. It may have developed from an ancient meeting place, or it may have been an entirely new creation. Whatever its origin, the lands around such a settlement were parcelled out among leading Saxons, who farmed and managed the land in ways which would endure for centuries.

The land which the Saxons took over was administered in hides. A hide was the amount of land which would sustain a family for a year; in other words, the amount of land which could be ploughed in a year by a team of eight oxen. This, of course, meant different things in different places and depended very much on the local climate and geology. But as a rough guide, a hide in today's terms, was somewhere between sixty and one hundred acres. In the same way, the shire was divided and administered in Hundreds, a Hundred being thought to represent one hundred families, though this forms part of an ongoing debate. Hundreds are thought to have been created in the reign of King Edgar (AD 957-975) and Sutton Veny was in the Hundred of Warminster, Warminster being a Royal Estate and a Minster town. Because of its close proximity to Heytesbury, also a Royal Estate and Minster, there has been much overlapping of parts of Sutton Veny. Over the centuries it has both lost and gained land around its boundaries and this may account for why the Hundreds of Heytesbury and Warminster often shared their moot place, or hundredal meeting place. This was almost certainly Moot Hill, the area also known as Mootlebury, the remains of which can still be seen today on the south side of the Warminster Bypass (No. 19). It was a small hill, rising above the river valley, approachable from the south, but probably with marshy land to the north where it sloped down to the Wylye. From here, the business of the Hundred would be conducted, in the open, with the representatives from each settlement, or later, each tithing, a sub-division of the Hundred.

Moot Hill, from the A36 Warminster Bypass

The earliest recorded Saxon association of Sutton Veny comes with the Anglo-Saxon Chronicle, an account of the history of England from the time of Christ until 1154, (the end of the Anarchy in England with the death of King Stephen). Though

Sutton Veny is not mentioned by name, the parish may contain landmarks which were of some significance during the reign of King Alfred. After his defeat by the Vikings in AD877, King Alfred took refuge in the area of the Somerset Levels known as Athelney. He built a stronghold there and remained with a band of faithful warriors until the following spring, when he rode with his men to Egbert's Stone (*Ecgbrytestan*). Much ink has been expended on where Egbert's Stone was, but on the balance of the evidence, it seems most likely to have been in the area of the 'Fort' at Six Wells Bottom at Stourhead. There the men of Somerset, Wiltshire and parts of Hampshire flocked to Alfred's banner. From here, the Anglo-Saxon Chronicle tells us, they moved off to Iley, where they spent the next day, presumably mustering more troops.

Some accounts refer to this place as Iley Oak, but the Chronicle gives only the name 'Iley', or *Iglea*. Eastleigh Wood in Sutton Veny was written '*Eleigh*' in 18th century documents and '*Illegh*' in one of the Wiltshire Civil Pleas of 1249. So whilst there is no conclusive evidence, it would seem probable that the meeting place of Alfred's troops was somewhere in this vicinity. The hundredal meeting place, Moot Hill, and the surrounding area of Mootlebury (see above) may have been a suitable place for the Alfredian troops to gather and would have been within, or very close to, the wood we now call Eastleigh. Certainly it would seem very likely that Alfred's army gathered within the boundaries of Sutton Veny on their way to Edington and its victory over the Vikings.

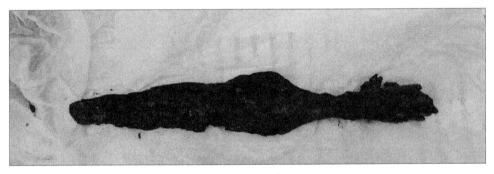

Anglo-Saxon spearhead, found locally and now in Warminster Museum

Under Alfred's rule, peace was restored to England and it is assumed that Sutton Veny, like most other settlements, continued its agricultural existence until the coming of the Normans in 1066. Alfred encouraged literature and the arts and is thought to have translated many texts into the vernacular. He even translated a document issued by Pope Gregory on 'Pastoral Care', of which he sent copies to all his dioceses, accompanied by an *aestel*, or manuscript pointer. Each *aestel* had an elaborately produced head, or terminal, usually decorated and jewelled, these being the only parts which have survived. Four *aestels* are known in England, the most famous being the Alfred Jewel, found in Somerset. In 1997, the head of an *aestel* was discovered near Cley Hill, again just outside the parish of Sutton Veny. It is not as elaborate as the Alfred Jewel, but it is, nonetheless, very beautiful, consisting of a rock crystal and a central lapis lazuli stone, all encased in gold wire and now known as the Warminster Jewel. It was purchased with the help of several grants and is now in the safe keeping of Salisbury Museum.

The Warminster Jewel
(By kind permission of Salisbury Museum)

MEDIEVAL PERIOD (AD 1066 – 1485)
By Sally Thomson

William the Conqueror's Great Survey of 1086

WITH THE COMING of the Normans, the Saxon way of life in England was to be gradually changed for ever, though it would take time for these changes to filter down to the ordinary man in the field and how far individual settlements like Sutton were affected by the new regime is difficult to assess. But in the years immediately following the Conquest, as William the Conqueror parcelled out the land, formerly held by Anglo-Saxon thegns (retainers) of their King, Edward the Confessor, they would certainly have been very aware of the change of lordship. In 1086, when William set in motion his great survey of the country, so that he might know how much tax he could bring into his coffers, the tenants on his manors might well have resented the intrusion into what livestock they owned and how much land they farmed. But since the king owned all the land and it was held of him by his earls and favourites, there was little the common people could do. The main part of the survey is now known as the Domesday Survey, written down by scribes criss-crossing the country over the course of about a year, gathering information. A second volume, the Exon Domesday, held slightly different information, which can be useful to historians, since it often fills in the gaps in our knowledge. Sutton Veny was one of those estates which appeared in both the Domesday Book and the Exon Domesday.

Manors

WILLIAM THE CONQUEROR's great survey of much of England was based on the content of manors. A manor in this context was not a building; it was more a state of being and comprised lands, estates and services, held of a lord, for which homage was made by the tenant of that lord. All land was owned by the king and he leased it out in parcels to his tenants-in-chief, usually Thegns during the Saxon period. Thegns, in turn, could sublet to under-tenants and there might be several layers of tenancy, thus sub-let, all tenants owing services and/or payment for their lands. A manor could be part of a parish, roughly contiguous with its borders; it could spread over several parishes; or there might be several manors within a parish, as in Sutton Veny.

A manor *house* was the building in which the lord of the manor lived, or, if he owned a number of manors, where his steward lived. In Saxon times, this would be the grandest building in the settlement and in time, it would be built of the best materials. There are two houses in Sutton Veny which contain medieval origins; one is the Old Manor House in Duck Street, which is essentially a mid-14th century hall house; the other is Polebridge Farmhouse.

Sutton Veny in Domesday Book

THERE WERE THREE holdings within Sutton at the time of the survey. One estate of four hides (about 480 acres, though this is not a precise quantity), was held in the time of King Edward by Alfwold and his sister. By 1086 this had been given to William son of Guy, who held it of King William. There was land for six ploughs, with four hides in lordship, or demesne, as it was known. There were two ploughs and four slaves in the demesne. This part of the estate contained six villagers and eight smallholders with four ploughs. There was a mill, in which the manor had a ⅔ share, which cost them 13s 4d. There were six acres of meadow and the pasture measured one league long by two furlongs wide, with woodland about the same amount. The value had been £8, but by 1086 was £10. This is the part of the manor which in later years came to be called Fenny Sutton.

Before 1066, Spirtes the priest held a second part of the settlement, which, with Fenny Sutton, was to become Great Sutton. This was given to Nigel the Physician by King William and he in turn leased it to the Abbey of St Mary of Montburg in the Départment of Manche in Lower Normandy. There was land for three ploughs, with two hides of the land, one plough and three slaves being in demesne. There were five villagers and five smallholders with two ploughs and the manor paid the remaining ⅓ of the rent of the mill, amounting to 6s 8d. There were three acres of meadow, pasture ½ league long and one furlong wide and woodland, one league long and one furlong wide. The value had been £4, but was now, at the time of the survey, £5. The following illustration shows the Domesday Book entry for this. Like all entries in Domesday, it was written in heavily abbreviated Latin; Sutton Veny appears in the first line as *SVDTONE* (Sutton).

Idẽ.N.teñ.IIII.hid̃ in *SVDTONE*.7 p̃ tanto geldb̃ T.R.E.Ťra.ẽ.III.caŕ. S MARIA de Monteburg teñ de Nig̃.De hac ťra s̃ in dñio.II.hidæ.

7 ibi.I.caŕ.7 III.ſerui.7 v.uiłłi 7 v.bord cũ.II.caŕ.Ibi ťcia pars molini redd̃.vI.ſot 7 vIII.den.7 III.ãc p̃ti.Paſtura dim̃ leũ lg̃.7 I.q̃ lat̃. Silua.I.leũ lg̃.7 I.q̃ lat̃.Valuit.IIII.lib̃.Modo.c.ſolid̃. Hæc.IIII.ⓂⓄ tenuit Spirtes p̃br T.R.E.

Printed transcription of the second entry for Sutton in Domesday Book

The third holding in Sutton was that which, in time, became Little Sutton, though it consisted of some five hides of land. In King Edward's time it had been held by one Cola, or Colo, but by 1086 it was held of the Conqueror by William de Mohun, who leased it out to Walter Husee, later Husey or Hussey. We learn Walter's surname from the Exon Domesday, in which it appears as *Hosatus*. At the survey, the holding had land for four ploughs, of which three hides and one virgate were in demesne, together with two ploughs and three slaves. There were also three villagers and six smallholders with two ploughs and it had the sole use of a mill, for which it paid 4s. There were four acres of meadow, two acres of woodland and the pasture measured ½ league long by 1 league wide. The value had been £4 and was now £5.

Sutton was now set to move into the later medieval world, where farming life itself would not be so very different, but laws would change and landholding would be subject to much tighter restrictions.

In time, the three tenants in chief of these manors conveyed or passed on their manors to descendants or relatives or even sold their manors to strangers. All these details are related in the Victoria County History of England for Wiltshire, volume 8. But it is a tortuous and complicated account and is best confined to a few family names, some of which persisted for centuries.

It would seem that Great Sutton consisted of two manors, Great Sutton and Fenny Sutton, centred around the old church of St Leonard. The third manor was Little Sutton, to the east of St Leonard's. Newnham did not appear in the records until the 13th century, when houses began to appear on the High Street, creeping northwards from Great Sutton up towards the Woolpack crossroads.

Nigel the Physician leased out Great Sutton to the Abbey of St Mary de Montebourg in Normandy, but soon afterwards it passed to Hamelin de Ballon. The Ballons held the manor from about 1090 -1275, followed by members of the Limesey, Cromhale, de Wauton and Daubeney families, until in the late 14th century it was acquired by Thomas Hungerford, the knight who fortified the Hungerford holding at

Farleigh, to create Farleigh Hungerford Castle. It passed down the Hungerford line until it reached Edward 'Spendthrift' Hungerford, when it was sold to Sir Stephen Fox, who split up the lands and sold them off in separate parcels.

Fenny Sutton, confusingly, was variously known as Great Sutton, Northcourt or South Morton, though these names did not persist. From William, son of Guy, it passed to Henry Newmarsh and through the female line to the Moels family until 1337. After this it was held by the Haudlo and Burnell families. In the 15th century it was, for a time, held directly of the King and then of the Dowager Countess of Wiltshire. Tenants in chief included the Lorty, Middleney and Ashton families. At one point, it was leased to the trustees of Alice Perers, the mistress of Edward III. One wonders if the people of Sutton knew that their lands were involved with the notorious mistress of their ageing king! In the late 16th century, the manor was sold to the Hungerfords and went the same way as Great Sutton.

Sutton Parva was given to William de Mohun by the Conqueror, and de Mohun leased it to Walter Hussee (Hussey) and his descendents. This arrangement lasted until 1242, when the manor was split between some of the tenants of Fenny Sutton, mentioned above – the Limesey, Cromhale and de Wauton families. Further splitting and conveyancing of the manorial lands occurred until eventually, most of Sutton Parva passed to Sir John de Kyngeston and his heirs. In 1521, the Lisle family, on the female side, inherited the manor. In 1539, due to a lack of heirs, it was divided between four cousins. Eventually, the shares in the manor were all reunited under the Marquis of Bath, which is why so many documents for Sutton Veny are now held at Longleat.

A manorial chapel

THE FREE CHAPEL of St Nicholas was situated within the manor of Sutton Parva, or Little Sutton. It may have been a chapel of ease, for the people of Sutton Parva were somewhat isolated from the main settlement and would have had a considerable way to travel to reach the parish church. A chapel of ease would have given them a place in which to hear Mass, but none of the ceremonies of Baptism, Marriage or burial could take place there. But it is more likely to have been a private chapel for the lord of the manor there. It is said that it was situated close to St Leonard's Church, which would make it an unlikely candidate for a chapel of ease. Whatever its original purpose, it had a very early origin, for in 1291 it was valued at £1 per annum and was held by John de Beswick.

An interesting occurrence took place in 1312, when on the 14 October, Thomas de Merlaunde, clerk, was presented to the chapel by Sir Thomas Kyngeston, in the presence of the Bishop of Sarum at Sonning, near Reading. On the 4 March, the following year, young Thomas was instituted as rector, despite his being only 14 years old; the Bishop made a special dispensation, because there was 'no cure there'; in other words, he did not have the responsibility of a parish. In fact he was probably a private chaplain to the lord of the manor, though he is not referred to as such. His institution took place at Potterne, where the Bishops of Sarum had a large palace.

The Kyngestons were also granted a dispensation for Divine service to be celebrated in the chapel and they continued as its patrons and presented until 1333. John Shaldon was the last cleric of the chapel, appointed in 1530 on the resignation of his predecessor, William May. Along with most other ecclesiastical institutions, St Nicholas's chapel was dissolved at the Reformation, its site lost and its existence known only through documents.

Taxation

FOR NATIONAL ADMINISTRATION purposes, the Hundreds of a shire were usually divided into tithings and so the name of Newnham first becomes known as a tithing. For some purposes, Sutton Veny was counted as a parish, and referred to just as 'Sutton'. But for others, the names of the tithings were used, as in the Tax List of 1332, where all three tithings are listed under the Hundred of Warminster. This tax was granted by Parliament to King Edward III, where the people outside towns and boroughs contributed a fifteenth on all their moveable goods; others paid a tenth. This was to aid the King in his war campaign against the French.

In Great Sutton (*Suttone Magna*), sixteen heads of households are recorded, the names of de Lortie and de Wautone being the two who paid the most, since they were tenants in chief. A total of 73s 5d was collected. Newnham (*Nywenham*) had only eight householders' names, Mounte being a name which would later lend itself to one of the mills. The total gathered was 35s 8½d. Little Sutton (*Suttone Parva*) contained the names of fourteen heads of houses, with a total collection of 47s 7¾d. John de Kyngestone paid the most, as one would expect.

Medieval farming

LIKE OTHER PLACES in the Wylye Valley, arable farming was carried out on a system of several open fields, which would be divided into strips, each strip being allotted to a tenant, who would plough, sow and cultivate the strip and finally harvest it. Not an ideal form of farming, for weed seeds from a careless peasant could spill over or blow onto a neighbour's strip, potentially ruining his precious crop. The way in which ploughing was carried out resulted in a ridge being created with a furrow on either side, acting as drains, what is now known as 'ridge and furrow'. The crop in each field was rotated each year, with one field being rested, or allowed to lie fallow, in order to recover, effectively putting out of use a large acreage for a whole year. In addition to tending his own strips, which would be scattered across the manor, the peasant would also have to provide a certain number of days' work on the lord's demesne, in other words, working the lord's private farm. Later, this service was commuted to a money payment, more convenient for all concerned.

In Sutton Veny, there were a number of large open fields divided into strips, and it appears that most of these fields were shared by the three manors, right up until the 17th century. There is a field in Sutton Veny, to the north of the Warminster A36 Bypass (No.20), in which have been noted the possible remains, though very faint, of ridge and furrow ploughing. The field is part of Kit Hurdles and Sutton Common North. Next to it is a field called The Leys. Leys was an old term meaning grassland, often arable laid to pasture and then ploughed up again.

In times of land shortage, when the population rose, such as just before the outbreak of the Black Death (1381), land would be tilled wherever a corner could be found. This often took the form of terraces, long strips of land running round the contours of a hillside, ploughed flat to accommodate the sowing of seeds. Two or three of these terraces would be made and they have left their mark on the landscape today, often called lynchets. There are many examples in the Wylye Valley and in particular, a very good set in Sutton Veny, on the north-west facing slope of Woodcombe Cleave, on the west side of Hill Road, and in the field called Glebe Hanging (No. 21).

Lynchets on Woodcombe Cleave

But the main farming activity for the settlement, as indeed it was for most of the Wylye Valley villages, was sheep farming. The downs provided perfect grazing during the day and the sheep in turn produced milk and fleeces. In medieval times, there was little demand for mutton or lamb, but milk and cheese from sheep were common products, while wool was the staple. From the 11th to the 15th centuries, English wool was paramount and was in great demand on the Continent and elsewhere, as well as within the country itself. Wool was used for all types of clothing, from the simple garb of the peasant, to the fine wool cloak of the lord. Most women spun wool and many dyed and wove it at home.

By the 15th century, all the demesne arable land was leased out for a rent of £7 per annum and the Hungerfords farmed the land only as a sheep farm. On a manorial basis, there was much coming and going of animals between Heytesbury, Sutton Veny and Farleigh Hungerford. Between 1417 and 1436 Sutton Veny contributed between 400 and 600 fleeces annually to the Hungerford wool stocks.

By the late 16th century, when the manors had more or less become farms, there was pasture for 500 sheep on the downs, with additional pasture for Fenny Sutton Farm on East and West Downs, on the heath 'under the wood' and West Heath, known as The Sands. The tenant farmer was also the bailiff and the manor was to provide hospitality at times when the manor courts met. Great Sutton had its own pasture for twelve sheep, with common of pasture for 640 sheep, a right shared between the demesnes of Great and Little Sutton.

In 1249, Adam de Jovene of Sutton was accused of sheep stealing and was taken to Salisbury Gaol. He managed to escape from there, but Nicholas of Haveresham, who was Sheriff of Wiltshire at the time, was held responsible. Adam was found guilty and was outlawed. Nicholas, no doubt, had to pay a hefty fine!

Surplus produce would be sold to others in need of the same and on 24 November 1298, a charter was issued for a Monday market to be held in Sutton Veny. At the same time, a charter was also issued for a fair to be held on 26 May, the feast of St Augustine. Both charters were granted by King Edward I to John de Kyngeston and both were to be held at the manor, presumably somewhere along Duck Street. There is no further evidence of either the market or the fair in the village, but this follows the pattern of many villages across England at the time. Numerous market charters were granted, but for one reason or another, the markets failed to keep going and were lost without trace. Sometimes it was because there was no main road nearby to catch the passing trade; or it may have been due to another market being held in a larger village or town close by. Sutton Veny was probably just too small to support either a market or a fair.

2
HOW THE VILLAGE EVOLVED

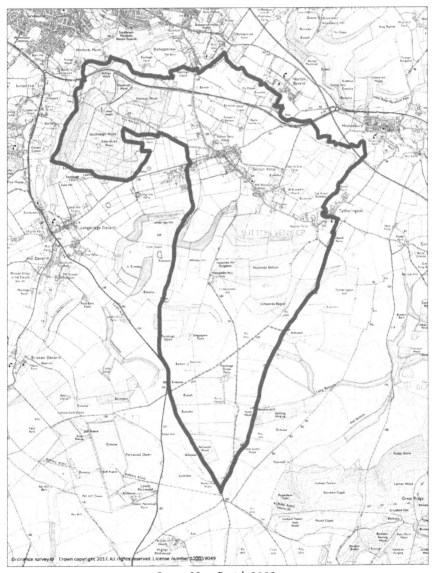

Sutton Veny Parish 2002

Layout of the Parish

SINCE THE 19TH CENTURY, the shape of civil parishes has been adjusted. In 1926 for example, the boundary of Sutton Veny parish was quite different.

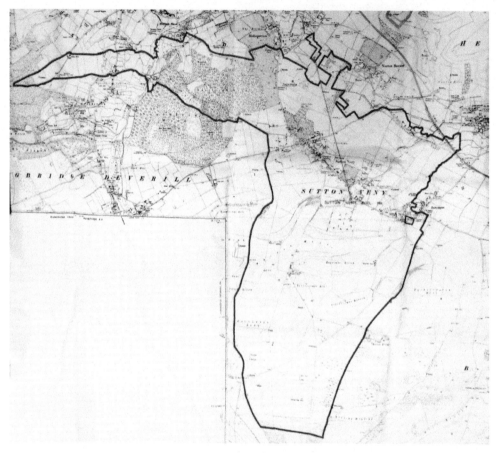

Sutton Veny Parish 1926

Today it is the shape of a broad question mark, roughly 3½ miles wide in the north, tapering 6 miles to a point at its southern tip. It covers about 6 square miles. There are two settlements, the village of Sutton Veny and the hamlet of Sutton Parva, the latter virtually merging with Tytherington village. They are both at the mouth of the wide Wylye Valley which is about 100m above sea level. The river itself is relatively narrow and, in practice, unnavigable for most of its length through the parish. On the north side, the ground rises steeply to Salisbury Plain whilst on the south side, it rises to chalk downland at Haycombe Hill Farm, 90m above the valley bottom. The highest point in the parish is nearby Whiten Hill, 201m above sea level.

Early buildings

M OST SETTLEMENTS in the country were built during the 9th and 10th centuries. When the Normans arrived, the local Saxon leaders were displaced and the Norman lords often adapted or built the manor houses, farmsteads and more often than not a stone church, sometimes replacing an earlier wooden structure.

While wanting to keep peasants some distance from the manor house itself, the lord often allowed them to build simple wattle hovels nearby which, when beyond repair, were simply taken down and rebuilt on the same site. Traders and craftsman would set up their businesses which, in addition to the church, became a focus for a community.

At the time of the Domesday Book there were three manors. As mentioned in chapter 1, 'a manor' included not only the actual building but also the lands, estates and services held by the lord. At the east end of the village there were the three manors of Fenny Sutton, Little Sutton and Great Sutton. In time the ownerships of these changed and eventually the two settlements of Little Sutton and Great Sutton emerged as separate entities. There is evidence of at least 12 wells in the vicinity of Great Sutton potentially providing a source of water to a community which may have served Polebridge Farm, Church Farm and the church. There could be a number of reasons why the people are no longer there, for instance fire, plague or perhaps something less dramatic such as unsuitable ground conditions. The hamlet of Little Sutton remained a separate entity until 1963.

Half a mile or so to the west was Newnham. There are records of this settlement going back to 1265 (and there is a little more about this in chapter 10 with the house called Manymans Mead). Newnham retained its individual identity until the middle of the 19th century.

Over time and with a gradual increase in personal prosperity, wattle houses were replaced with more substantial structures built of local sandstone. Dressed stone was brought over from Chilmark and Frome for the more prosperous. Subsequently, bricks became more widely available from brickworks at Crockerton.

Newnham developed because it is at the crossroads of two local routes: the winding valley road from Warminster to Salisbury and the Deverill road crossing the river to Heytesbury and onwards along the dryer route to Salisbury (now the A36). The constant flow of travellers passing through Newnham encouraged the expansion of the hamlet and with it, simple shops, trades and not unsurprisingly, a public house. The arrival of the Everett family in the 19th century, with their acquisition and significant development of the Greenhill estate, contributed to the increasing local prosperity.

How the name of Sutton Veny evolved

'SUTTON' IS A COMMON English place name derived from the Saxon word *sud* meaning southward, southern or in the south etc. The opposite is of course *nor*, ie northward (as in Norton Bavant).

The name Sutton 'Parva' (originally Little Sutton) is derived from the Latin *parvus* meaning small.

'Great' Sutton comes from Sutton Magna (from the Latin *magnus* meaning large).

The word 'Veny' is likely to be a derivation of the *fen*. Being at the bottom of a flat river valley, the land was marshy, ie fenny. Hence the emergence of the name Sutton Venny and subsequently Sutton Veny.

One of the first recorded uses of 'Veny' was in the *Valor Ecclesiasticus* (a valuation made at the dissolution of the monasteries), when it was recorded in 1535 as Veny Sutton.[1]

The settlement of Newnham plays no part in the origin of the village's name.

Maps

THE EARLIEST PLAN giving a clear layout of the village was prepared in 1788 as evidence in a dispute between Longleat's Lord Weymouth and Sir Walter Long of Polebridge Farm. It was about the ownership of an elm tree that stood on Newnham Green at the crossroads of High Street and the Deverill Road.[2]

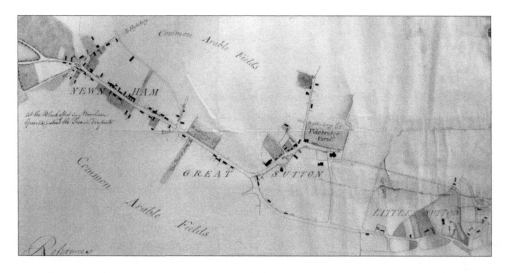

Lawsuit 1788

At the end of the 19th century, mapmaking was still in its infancy. Buildings and other features were by and large illustrative because accurate surveying was a costly process. As a consequence, maps that were commissioned were made for a specific client; maps over a general region were unusual.

The earliest map of Wiltshire was by Andrews and Dury, and published in 1773 (revised in 1801). The majority of the dwellings and villages are only stylised illustrations. To defray the cost of publication, private mapmakers relied on selling them, effectively by seeking sponsorship from those who were likely to pay ie wealthy landowners. This explains why, for example, Heytesbury House is shown in such detail, as well as, although not to such a degree, the intriguingly named 'Who Will House' (now Eastleigh Farm) near Bishopstrow.

However, while accurate detail is missing, the map is useful in giving the general layout of local villages and how they sit in the landscape in relation to each other. This particular map from the 1801 edition has had colouring added; the routes in red are principal roads, and the green and yellow lines are the boundaries of hundreds (referred to in the Early History Saxon chapter).

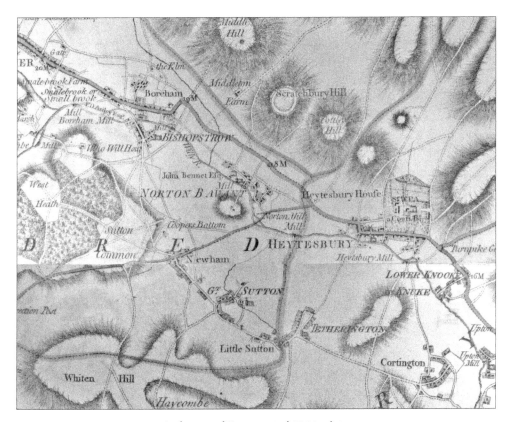

Andrews and Dury revised 1810 edition

Enclosures

THE FIRST MORE accurate and relatively detailed map of the area comes at the end of the 18th century with the Enclosure Acts. These Acts resulted in a fundamental reshaping of much of the countryside. The ancient method of arable husbandry was by the Open Field system – each church, manor or village had several hundred acres which were divided into narrow strips for cultivation, similar in some ways to the present allotment system. This was generally an inefficient use of land. For example peasants often had individual strips scattered over a wide area, there was infestation of weeds from the strip of a careless adjoining occupier, and there was virtually no control of grazing cattle.

Over the years, landowners had individually carried out their own rationalisations and by the end of the 18th century the principle was formalised across the country by a series of Enclosure Acts. The Enabling Act for Sutton Veny was passed in 1798. This was for *dividing and allotting in severalty the open and common fields and Downs, Common Meadows, Common Pastures and Commonable Places within or belonging to the Parish of Sutton Veny in the County of Wiltshire.*

The transition process was put into effect following an examination of submissions made to a panel of commissioners specially appointed by local landowners and occupiers. Their decision on future land ownership was recorded by an Award registering their decisions.

The Sutton Veny Award was published in 1804 and the 29 page document includes maps illustrating the land awarded to the new owners, two of whose names remain familiar today: Best (the Lane) and Barter (the forge in Duck Street). The red buildings on the map are houses.

An enlarged section of the map showing Duck Street gives an interesting perspective of the roads, tracks and paths. It also shows the groundwater rising at Springhead and collecting at a pond in the middle of the street as it made its way down to the river at Mount Mill.

Vestry and Parish Council

AS A PAYMENT for his services, a rector would receive tithes which were one-tenth of the produce of the land such as crops, eggs, cattle and timber. Under the Act, this was replaced by cash. Rector Brounker Thring did quite well – being awarded not only cash, but also over 600 acres of land, enlarging the Glebe Estate to 830 acres.

From Anglo-Saxon times, the inhabitants of a community had carried out their collective business at town or village meetings in one form or another. Their function

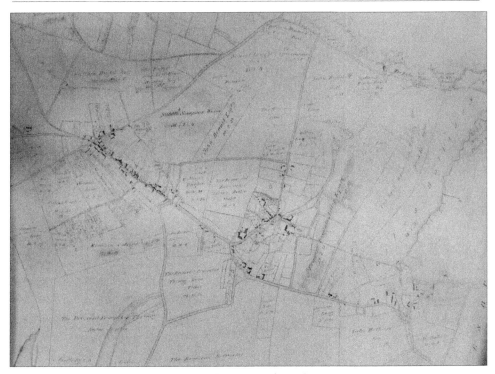

Enclosure Award 1804

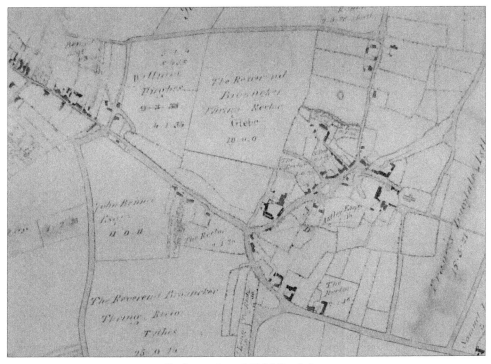

Enclosure Award 1804 Duck Street

and purpose altered through the ages with ecclesiastical parishes and manors often sharing the same boundaries. Initially, the manor was the principal component of local administration and of justice in the rural economy, but gradually the Church replaced the role of the manorial court.

The Reformation in the 16th century led to a new form of parish meeting. It dealt with both civil and ecclesiastical affairs and was supervised by the parish priest, as he was probably the best educated inhabitant. The meetings were held in the parish church or more particularly, the vestry, from which they derived their name. Since there was no other form of administration, the duties of the Vestry increased. It became, for instance, responsible for appointing parish officials such as the Parish Clerk, the Overseers of the Poor and the Sexton.

By the early 19th century their responsibilities had extended still further in to the realm of civil administration: keeping of the peace, the repression of vagrancy, the relief of destitution, the mending of roads, the suppression of nuisances. It also commissioned, for instance, the 1871 review of the sanitary state of the village outlined in chapter 3.

The secular and ecclesiastical duties were finally separated in 1894 with the introduction of a system of elected rural (and urban) councils, leaving Parish Vestries with only the management of church affairs. For the village, the next level down from

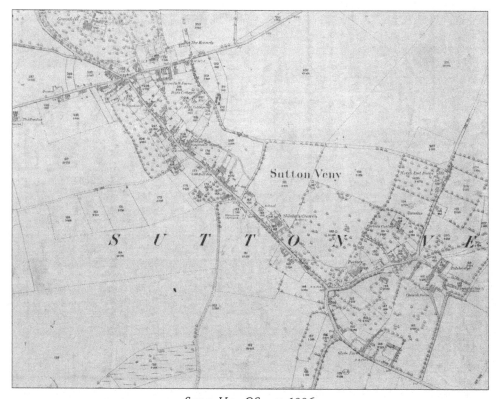

Sutton Veny OS map 1886

Warminster Rural District Council was Sutton Veny Parish Council and its first meeting
took place in the National Schoolroom adjoining Chapel Drain on 3rd January 1895.

Street numbering

A S T H E N U M B E R of houses increased, formal addresses became a necessity. It is
not known for certain which authority was behind Sutton Veny's house numbering
system, but it came into use in about 1918. Apart from some minor exceptions, the
official who allocated the numbers seems to have applied the 'right-hand side-rule' i.e.
numbering only houses on the right-hand side of all the roads; effectively he followed
the star shaped route shown below.

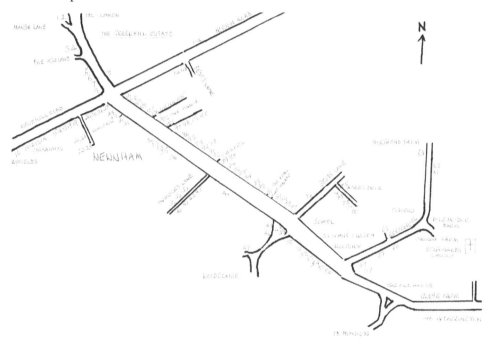

Street numbering route

Whilst producing a logical sequence on one side of the road, it still sometimes
baffles strangers and delivery van drivers. A simple example can be found in the High
Street: opposite No. 111 is No. 30 and No. 27 is round the corner from 24 and so on. A
number of householders compound the confusion by making no reference at all to their
house number, but merely refer to a house by its name.

3
THE VILLAGE FRAMEWORK

Routeways, roads and tracks

THE PREHISTORIC COUNTRYSIDE of Britain was criss-crossed by routeways. They were mainly on higher ground and provided a route for people to travel from one settlement to another, driving stock to fresh pasture or for the more adventurous, a long-distance route much further afield.

Trade routes also began to open up and it is possible that the Wylye Valley would have been an important route for the growing trade in raw materials such as copper and tin to make bronze, and for the export of surplus grain. The Sutton Veny area also lay along the line of several other important communication and trade routes that may have had their origins in the Neolithic period.

Many of these trackways have persisted for millennia; some now lie beneath our major roads, while others remain as quiet tracks and lanes. The prehistoric Great Ridgeway passing through Sutton Veny has already been described in chapter 1 and illustrated on the map of Prehistoric and Historic Features. Whilst trackways such as these formed part of a much wider network, the routes that some followed will have had an impact on nearby settlements, and an understanding of how they fit into the wider picture is useful.

All three tracks more or less converge at the southernmost point of Sutton Veny parish at ST898366, before heading towards Pertwood and East Knoyle. At the convergence they are crossed by what may be yet another important routeway – the so-called Groveley Ridgeway – which runs east-west along the watershed between the Wylye and Nadder valleys. It was once part of a through-way that began at the Kent coast and came eventually to the Mendips and the Bristol Channel. However, this is not as straightforward as it would at first seem.

In Saxon times, routeways tended to come down off the high ground and to follow lower valley tracks. This may have been due to extensive draining of marshy areas in valley bottoms opening up new tracks, at least in summer, and enabling cattle to be grazed in the lush meadows by streams and rivers.

Prior to the 17th century roads were often little more than tracks, as they had been for hundreds of years. In wet weather the ground would become almost impassable, since only rudimentary attempts were made to improve surface water drainage. During the winter, travel through the countryside would become extremely difficult making the transport of food and goods almost impossible; in effect, parts of the countryside virtually closed down.

Back Lane

From Saxon times the way between Warminster and Salisbury took travellers along the drier, lower slopes of Salisbury Plain. This may have helped Codford and Heytesbury to develop into prosperous communities, but being on the south side of the river, Sutton Veny and Sutton Parva did not benefit from this route and the absence of significant numbers of travellers passing through had a detrimental effect on the economy of both settlements. As a consequence, their communities survived, rather than thrived.

In time, the local wealth began to grow and in common with other communities, the shared prosperity came primarily from the production of timber, grain, meat and above all, wool.

By the latter part of the 17th century the volume of cart, wagon and carriage movements increased to such an extent that the poor state of repair of roads was having an effect not only on the locality, but on the country as a whole. It usually fell to wardens

Although most domestic wells have now been filled in, several still exist. The potability of the water of one at the top of the village was tested in the mid 1980s. The result was that whilst not particularly palatable, it was unlikely to poison anyone. However, drinking the water was not recommended because modern digestive systems are unable to cope with it untreated.

to make sure that roads were regularly mended, which meant using parish funds – and these were often scarce.

Turnpiking was an attempt to force the road user, rather than the local inhabitants, to bear the cost of road improvements and maintenance. This was facilitated by individual Acts of Parliament giving local trustees powers to levy tolls to fund the works on specific stretches of road. These stretches were called turnpikes, after the gate or pole, which blocked the road until the toll was paid.

The process of selecting stretches of roads for turnpiking depended on several factors, for example the nature of the soil and the gradients, and whether labour was available for maintenance.

Two turnpike routes passed through Sutton Veny. The first was authorised by an Act in 1727 and was for a series of roads radiating out from Warminster Town Hall. One of these extended to Heytesbury with a branch threading from Boreham down the valley to Corton, passing through Sutton on its way. On 21 March 1833, the Devizes and Wiltshire Gazette, reported a meeting to ...*order and direct that a toll gate or bar be erected and set up in the parish of Sutton Veny across that part of the turnpike road leading from Warminster to Sutton Veny called Market Lane, and near or contiguous to certain cottages late of Ann Hinton, spinster, deceased.* There is no evidence where this was or indeed that a toll gate was ever built.

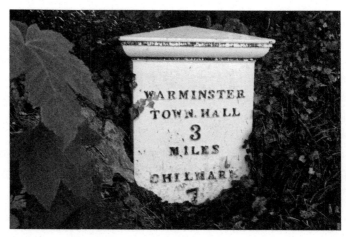

Milestone

The second road was authorised in 1792. It came from Bruton, passed through Maiden Bradley and entered Sutton Veny at the High Street/Woolpack crossroads. Again, the position of the tollhouse is not known but the road went on to Norton Bavant to join the turnpike road from Warminster to Heytesbury.

From 1750 trusts were required to erect milestones indicating the distance to main towns on the road. Two can still be seen in the parish; one at the Common and this one on the High Street opposite the school. They are both cast iron, clearly a replacement of the original.

With trade increasing significantly as the Industrial Revolution gathered pace and with the massive development of the rail system, the accumulated mortgage debts had rendered the majority of the trusts across the country insolvent; road maintenance was subsequently taken over by local councils.

Railways

I N 1851, the Great Western Railway opened its station at Warminster as the terminus of its branch from Westbury on its Wiltshire, Somerset and Weymouth route. This was subsequently extended to Salisbury in 1856, and a station was built near Heytesbury – just two miles from Sutton Veny. Originally just a single track, the line was doubled eastwards in 1899 and then westwards to Warminster the following year.

Passenger numbers for the period 1903 to 1933 suggest its busiest period was the turn of the century but it subsequently declined rapidly in the late 1920s. The handling of general freight, coal and 'other minerals' also gradually reduced over a similar period. However, although the freight of cattle was largely from the cattle market at Warminster, Heytesbury supported several elements of Sutton Veny's economy. In time the station was no longer viable, and it closed in 1955.

Drainage

D URING THE LATE 19th and early 20th centuries most rural communities had no truly effective method of dealing with human and domestic waste. In Sutton Veny one or two of the better houses had water closets draining into carefully cemented cesspits, with the contents being pumped onto the garden as manure. But the general system of disposing of human waste was by privy and pit, bricked or unbricked, open or covered, and it was emptied once or twice a year.

Domestic water was simply thrown outside and found its way into crude channels each side of the road. Whilst some liquids percolated into the ground, but the residue remained to form a festering scum. The air outside, particularly in the High Street, would have been more or less permanently unpleasant, and foetid in hot weather.

The health of the villagers was generally good, but by 1868 the Parish Vestry became concerned about the increase in outbreaks of fevers with *a good many of the children pale and sickly-looking with cases of deafness, dropsical* [enormous ankles] *and glandular swellings found among those recovering from scarlatina.*

Because the High Street was a turnpike, the turnpike commissioners agreed to give £25 towards improving the surface drains on condition that the Vestry paid an equal sum. They agreed to raise this by public subscription. A house to house inspection was carried out , accompanied by the Parish Medical Officer, the Inspector of Police in Warminster and a splendidly named official, the 'Inspector of Nuisances', Mr Abbot.

In 1868 several improvements were proposed and Mr Abbot was authorised to see that they were carried out. The Vestry ordered the laying of new gutters each side of the High Street in the form of a shallow open trough, these were made from three rows of bricks with slanted sides, traces of which can still be seen.

1868 brick open trough

The gutters were never cleaned properly and as a consequence they regularly overflowed and foul water seeped into the walls and under the doors of adjoining cottages. Outside the Bell Inn there was, until recently, a urinal (by today's pillar box) discharging into the drain. To add to the misery, privies and pits sometimes overflowed into cottages and wells.

By 1871 there had been a marked downturn in the health of the population, with 80 cases of scarlet fever and 12 deaths. An official of the Medical Department of the Local Government Board, Dr Hubert Airy, was tasked to enquire and report on the sanitary state of the Parish. He found that *whilst the water supply in the village was generally good, the disposal of excrement and household slops was a matter of significant concern.* For example:

. . . Throughout the village the nasty custom prevails of emptying slops (seldom sewerage or urine) on the rudely-paved space beside the well. Most of the fluid runs off by a gutter of some kind, but a residuum is constantly left to soak and stagnate between the rough irregular cobble-stones that serve as a pavement. An open gutter, of cobble-stones or bricks, leads the slops and yard drainage into the street.

…a well attached to a cottage at the side of a farmyard (known as Randall's), where it was said that in summer the well-water came to resemble the farmyard drainage in colour and smell…

…and in other parts of the village there are wells exposed to danger of contamination at much shorter distances, one five yards from a privy, another four yards from a nasty leaky urinal.

. . . At the back of a row of four cottages (Carpenter's), I found the single privy about 4 yards from the dwellings, recessed into the sloping bank of garden ground behind. Naturally, the pit was flooded, and the privy floor was covered with filth, which overflowed and ran down to the cottage back-doors and along the foot of the house wall to the roadside gutter. In another part of the village there is a ditch full of stagnant filth from a privy bordering a piece of ground chosen for the site of a new village school.

The report identified a number of reasons for the spread of the diseases:

. . . The children were constantly brought into contact among themselves in their crowded bedrooms and in the village schools. In the bedroom the fever spread among members of the same family; in the school it spread among families of the same religious denomination. At first the outbreak was mainly confined to families sending children to the 'church school' at the present time it is confined to families sending children to the 'chapel school'. This fact alone is enough to show how large a share the school-contact has had in promoting the spread of the disease.

A child named Viney caught the fever at school; she was nursed by a girl named Parker, who took the fever and went home. There, while in the height of the fever, the girl Parker was visited by the maid servant from a house where there was a family of young children. Within a fortnight four of the young children were down with scarlet fever, and one died.

Dr Airey's first recommendations dealt with general precautions to prevent the spread of disease by opening windows to create a through-draft, the use of disinfectants and safeguards against contamination and the cross-infection within families, school children and the general population.

His second was the removal of privies and other sources of contamination from the vicinity of houses and wells, with the adoption of a regular system of excrement removal and the proper management of slop water. The latter was to be implemented by the construction of a main sewer down the street. It was to be properly ventilated, at a proper depth to receive slops from houses on either side by house drains. It was to have proper gratings to exclude solid refuse. This main sewer would need to be regularly flushed at the top of the street.

The Vestry immediately agreed to carry out all the proposals in the report. However, nothing seems to have been done and even after Warminster Rural District Council had assumed maintenance responsibility in 1897, the gutters had neither been cleared nor repaired.

And so the situation appears to have remained until the troops arrived at the outbreak of the First World War. In 1916, sickness once again became an issue. This time, the finger of blame pointed at the huge camp at the top of the village. The Parish Council complained to the Rural District Council who complained to the Army who reported to the War Office. The response of the latter was that the wells in Sutton Veny were, and always had been, liable to contamination because the improvements planned by the Vestry 25 years previously, had not been carried out; and in any event 'the Camp sewage was treated and satisfactorily managed'; in short, it's not *our* fault. In reality it would appear[3] that overflow pipes from the Army sewage beds behind the Deverill Road cottages had occasionally been opened, flooding nearby fields and polluting wells.

Water

THE DISAGREEMENT FLOWED back and forth with the newly formed Sutton Veny Water Works Committee joining the dispute. Water samples were taken from wells in various parts of the village and sent for independent analysis. Eleven were condemned outright and in three more, the water was deemed unfit for human consumption. The committee once more pointed to the camp's sewage system. They drew attention to the indisputable fact that many soldiers regularly visited the village, particularly the public houses and canteens, and were drinking the fouled water to the detriment of their health and their potential operational military effectiveness.

This seems to have done the trick and the War Office agreed, without accepting responsibility for the contamination, to extend their own water supply from Greenhill down into the village. The civilian population at that time was 566 but only 500 were to be supplied with water at a rate of 20 gallons per head per day. This was to be a temporary measure which would only continue for a period of six months after the Declaration of Peace.

Water was not to be piped into the houses themselves, but supplied instead to seven standpipes. In the High Street these were located at The Woolpack, Little

Newnham, Dymocks Lane, The Bell Inn and Hill Road. When the Woolpack was rebuilt in 1931, the standpipe was moved a few yards to the neighbouring Jessamine Cottage.

In the event, the supply continued until well after the cessation of hostilities and it was not until 1920 that the War Department gave notice that the supply of water would be discontinued in May 1922. This was adequate time for an alternative to be secured – or was it?

There followed a series of complex negotiations. Basil Hoare, who then owned Greenhill House, agreed to give land with access for a pumping house, a well and storage tank in return for the council supplying his land and houses with free water.

Woolpack standpipe

It was the view of the Ministry of Health that the cost of the water supply should be borne by the Rural District Council. In addition they would only agree to a supply no further than Duck Street; Sutton Parva was excluded from the scheme. The reason for this is not known and is all the more curious since their only source of water came from a polluted well. It may be that their supply was planned to come from the Tytherington borehole above that village.

With the water supply settled, there was still the question of drains and sewage. In 1972 a Warminster RDC sewage disposal scheme was put forward for the 13 parishes of the Upper Wylye Valley. It was approved in principle by the Department of the Environment, the sites of pumping stations were identified, and preparatory drawings and contracts prepared.

Three months later, the Rural District Council was abolished and their place was taken by West Wiltshire District Council. Responsibility for sewage treatment was taken over by the newly formed Wessex Water. They did not include the Wylye Valley scheme in their Five Year Plan so the whole project came to a halt.

Matters moved forward a little in 1976 when Sutton Veny Parish Council once more raised the question of mains drainage. Whilst there was no legislative requirement for a Water Authority or a District Council to provide new sewers, the scheme was re-examined. Estimates suggested that each household would have to contribute £400 – £600 plus the cost of filling defunct septic tanks. This was considered to be too expensive (it is not known by whom and on whose authority). The Wylye Valley Sewerage and Sewer Disposal Scheme went ahead without Sutton Veny.

In the 1998 the Sutton Veny Appraisal (chapter 7) was held to give people an opportunity to express their views on various aspects of village life. One question, *Would you support the introduction of mains drainage into the village?* drew a response of 60% in favour. There the matter remains.

Electricity

IT IS NOT KNOWN for certain when mains electricity was laid to the village but the Parish Council minutes of 13 March 1933 note their welcoming *the advance of electricity but the erection of poles should be limited and cables should be laid underground.* A fortnight later the council reported that the Wessex Electricity Company would be making arrangements with the owners of properties about erecting poles on their land; there was no mention of cables being underground.

4
PLACES OF WORSHIP

ST LEONARD'S CHURCH

An early history of building

The shell of St Leonard's today

IN ANCIENT TIMES this part of the valley may have been marshy to the north with fertile grazing land spreading south and up to the downs. The site of St Leonard's Church is higher than much of the immediately surrounding land and it is conceivable (although there is no evidence) that, with the nearby ancient burial sites, this piece of land *might* have had some ritual significance. It is certainly true that with the arrival of Christianity, churches were often built on the sites of earlier temples in an attempt to ease the introduction of Christianity to the population.

It is known that there was a Norman church on this site because there are signs of a Norman arch in the North door (albeit now heavily stylised). It is possible it was built by a Norman lord usurping the occupying Saxon nobleman who might have built an earlier wooden church.

St Leonard's 1866

The Norman arch

The first mention of the church is several hundred years later in Patent Rolls in 1220.[4]

In the same way it is written by the aforesaid James de Poterne, John Mautravers, Hugh le Droeis and Robert Maudit, of the last assizes presentors to the church of Sutton, taken at Wilton from St Michael's Day for 15 days, that Nicholas de Limese and Margaret his wife, Dionisia and Florence sisters of Margaret, have called an assize against the Prior of Bergaveni [Abergavenny]. Witnessed by H. etc. at Wilton, the 13th day of September. By the same. And the sheriff of Wiltshire is commanded, that the assize shall come to be made before them.

The earliest record of a rector is John de Bradeham in 1297 but apart from that, nothing more is known about the building or the congregation it served. The first surviving record of a baptism is that of William Snelger in 1570, and the first burial of John Bendall a few years earlier in 1564.

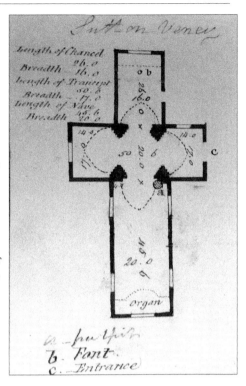

Interior layout

There are traces of substantial buttresses being built in the 13th and 16th centuries, and in 1698 there is reference to building work to support the tower. Clearly, structural stability had been an issue over the centuries.

The building was a cruciform design with a nave, chancel, north and south transepts and a central tower.

Sittings

INITIALLY, IF CONGREGATIONS wished to sit down during services they had to bring their own stools. Later they were provided with seats or benches, and gradually pews were introduced. Some areas of the church were considered to be more desirable because they offered a better view of the service and gave individuals more prominence than others, and so the concept of reserved spaces developed and with it, the notion of having a private box. This privilege was sometimes granted to benefactors, or came with the ownership of property, or was simply purchased. The boxes are clearly visible in the illustration overleaf.

1866 Interior from an original painting

The building today

E VEN AS A SHELL, a sense of St Leonard's past continues to linger.

Coat of Arms

THE ROYAL ARMS will often be found on boards fixed to the wall of churches. They were erected as tokens of loyalty to the Crown and obedience to the sovereign as head of the church.[5]

These are the Coats of Arms of Great Britain and repainted in modern times. An interesting feature is in the escutcheon (the central circular element). The bottom right-hand quarter of this contains the White Horse of Hanover and the top right-hand quarter (with a blue background) contains the three lilies of France. These two emblems did not appear in Royal Arms after George III's death in 1820, so it is likely that whilst these arms were originally painted as those of George III, a parsimonious churchwarden had the additional two elements added at the accession of the Prince Regent as George IV.

Coat of Arms

The Font

RECENT EXPERT OPINION suggests that it is possibly constructed from three separate fonts over the years and is no earlier than Norman and may be early 13th century.[6]

The Font   *The Axford Font*

In his short history of the church of St. John the Evangelist, and the parish of Sutton Veny, Roland Desch (Rector 1970) refers to *a battered Norman font found in a farmyard in the village*. The font above would seem to have been the original one, and some interesting facts relating to it were found in the correspondence of Arthur Sewell who was Rector before the First World War.

It appears that the original font had passed into the hands of a villager, John Randall in about 1825, possibly when it had been replaced by a modern one at about the turn of the 19th century. After the old font had been rediscovered in the farmyard, the parish gave the 'modern' one to a Rev. F.J.H.Axford, who at the time, was Rector of St. John's, Cornwallis, Nova Scotia, whilst he was on a visit to Sutton Veny (his birthplace). He took it away to his parish and it is now in the Church of St Thomas, Kingsport, Nova Scotia.[7]

Wall painting

THE ORIGIN OF this fragment is unknown and whilst it is believed to have originated in the ruined nave, it is not as old as it purports to be. It is probably 18th century and would have formed part of the decorative border to a painted text such

Wall painting

as the Ten Commandments. The ochre part at the bottom looks to be part of a separate scheme possibly painted later over the top.[8]

The bier

THE BIER WAS MADE in the 1890s by two brothers, Joseph and John Barter, who were builders, blacksmiths, wheelwrights and undertakers in Duck Street. They used it to take coffins to the chancel at St Leonard's which by then was used as a mortuary.

William Barter was the Sexton and his daughter remembered that as a child she was given rides on the empty bier by her uncles when they returned it to their workshop after their sombre task was done.

It was last used in 1968 for the funeral of Charles Goodall when his coffin was wheeled from his home at the Manor, across the park to St John's. It is now kept in the Chancel.

Tom Wigmore known as 'Blind Tom', lived in one of the terrace of cottages

The bier

opposite the lane to St Leonard's. He tolled the church bell when a parishioner died: three for a deceased man, two for a woman and one for a child. People then counted the number of rings, one for each year of life.

Graveyard ground level

The graveyard

AT A GLANCE, the reason for the structural issues that plagued the building seem perfectly clear – it was sinking. In fact this is not the case; it isn't that the building has *sunk* but rather that the surrounding ground level has *risen* as result of the re-use of graves over the centuries.

We know from the Burial Register that between 1638 and 1864, there were an average of 10 deaths a year, or 100 each century. On this premise, over the 500 year history of the building there have been roughly 5,000 burials. This figure is perfectly feasible given the high mortality rate from famine, plague and unrecorded infant deaths. Either way it certainly gives a broad indication of the remains now resting here. Whilst today's burials take place in St John's, very occasionally some are in St Leonard's. In 1983, Leslie Addington and David Norris had the foresight to record the surviving monuments before they were obliterated.[9]

The replacement debate

IN 1831, AFTER a six-year programme of repair and restoration and the addition of an organ and gallery, the building was believed to be in a condition to face a long future. However, within 30 years more repairs were needed. In the early 1800s an architect was called in to restore it and he advised that the church should be abandoned and a new one erected on a drier and more central site.[10]

It was with this background that Joseph and Frances Everett of Greenhill offered to fund an entirely new church. The village community by that time was no longer concentrated around Duck Street but towards Newnham – and the perfect place for a new church would be on Glebe land to the west of the Rectory, beside the High Street.

The prospect of abandoning St Leonard's did not meet with wholehearted approval for it had, after all, been the focus of worship for countless generations. Understandably feelings ran deep and the debate would have been passionate. There are suggestions that the repairs to St Leonard's *were* practical and perhaps they *could* have been put into effect, were it not for the Everett family's irresistible offer to build a new church.

Whatever the opinions for and against, George Powell, the 34th Rector of Sutton Veny, was the last of St Leonard's church and the first Rector of St John the Evangelist.

The end of an era

WITH THE COMPLETION of St John's in 1868, St Leonard's continued to deteriorate. The chancel remained consecrated and was used as a mortuary chapel but the remainder was abandoned. Some stone from the nave and transept was

The overgrown ruin, 1967

re-used in the village, particularly to build the new school. The roofless walls of the nave were left standing derelict and overgrown.

In about 1938, the Rev. E.D. Long (who had been born in the village) and Mr Hurst-Brown, gave St Leonard's a new altar, oak candlesticks and crucifix. To mark their dedication, Holy Communion was celebrated there.

In 1967, the Rector Ronald Desch, writing in the Sutton Veny and Norton Bavant Newsletter, raised an awareness of the building's condition. Whilst occasional services had been held in the chancel, the last had been three years previously, *with worshippers standing in pools of water from rain which had driven in through a hole in the roof and had become too dangerous to use. It was going to rack and ruin.* He commented that the church was part of a heritage passed on from previous generations and that there was a responsibility towards it. He said in the article that he planned to spend a day making a start on tackling the churchyard himself and would welcome help. Eight men, two women, 14 children and four teenagers from the youth club came to help.

The building was declared redundant in 1970 and it came under the care and maintenance of the Churches Conservation Trust the following year. It is still occasionally used for services.

ST JOHN THE EVANGELIST

A new church

JOSEPH AND FRANCES EVERETT of Greenhill (now Sutton Veny House) offered to fund a new church dedicated to St John the Evangelist, to replace St Leonard's. Joseph died in 1865 before building had begun; his widow went on to build it in his memory.

The site of the new church in the High Street was in a more central position than St Leonard's and offered a far more convenient pedestrian access and parking for carriages. There was also ample room for a churchyard. The reduction of an 800 yard walk to church for most villagers would have been welcomed.

The building

THE BUILDING WAS designed by John Loughborough Pearson, one of the country's most eminent and prolific architects, having designed a large number of notable churches and buildings. He was also entrusted with the care of many of the country's most distinguished cathedrals and historic buildings; he was well chosen.

St John's is on the Statutory List of Buildings of Special
Architectural or Historic Interest as Grade 1. That is a building
of exceptional interest and stands with, for example, Longleat,
Stourhead and Wilton houses. The Victorian Society regard it
as *one of the finest examples of a Victorian village church.*[11]

To the casual observer the church has a number of
interesting features. The most striking is the spire which,
standing 134 feet above the top of the tower, appears
somewhat thickset and truncated. Pearson had originally
intended it to be 20 feet higher but doubted the foundations
could carry the additional weight of stone. Whilst he *could*
have miscalculated the weight of the church spire to the extent
that he felt obliged to reduce its height, it is curious that an
architect of his eminence would have made such a significant
miscalculation. An alternative explanation might be that as
John Loughborough Pearson

the work progressed, the costs had spiralled from an initial £3,000 to over £7,000;
savings had to be made. However, having engaged such an architect, using the best
materials and completing the building to an exacting 18 month deadline, perhaps it was
inevitable that the building would be over budget.[12]

Another interesting feature of the church is that the building is not built on the
usual east-west axis. The east window faces south-east, so that it aligns with sunrise at
the winter solstice and on the following six days (which include Christmas and the
patronal festival of St John the Evangelist, 27th December). It follows that the west
window glows in the midsummer sunset.[13] It is a matter for conjecture whether the
alignment of the building is the result of a conscious decision or merely a coincidence
that it also follows the run of the High Street for all to admire. Either way, the building
sits comfortably on the site and adds a quiet dignity to the village.

No copies of the building drawings are known to have survived but the
foundations would have been hand dug, potentially anywhere between 10 and 30 ft.
deep. As usual, the trenches in which the foundations were laid, were wider than the
final walls and filled with a mix of flints and lime which were rammed down. It was a
huge and laborious task.

Foundation stone

THE WARMINSTER HERALD noted that the first clod of earth was dug on 7th
May 1866 with the foundation stone being laid a few weeks later on 29th May. It
noted particularly, that the family wanted the event to be as quiet, unostentatious and
private as possible. There were no invitations outside the parish. However, even then all
the principal local families were there together with a large crowd of parishioners. Lunch

was served in the Duck Street Rectory (today the Manor) and afterwards a procession to the site was accompanied by the village choir and children, As the day itself was the anniversary of the restoration of King Charles II, everyone wore oak leaves.[14]

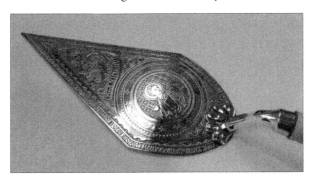

Foundation stone trowel

The Rector read the Service and at the appointed moment, Mrs Everett was handed a silver trowel to spread the mortar before the stone was lowered into place. In a cavity of the stone, a glass bottle had been inserted containing coins of the realm and a parchment with the inscription:

Church of St John the Evangelist, Sutton Veny.
To the Glory of God, for the good of men.
And in pious memory of JOSEPH EVERETT of Greenhill, in this Parish.
Frances Alice, his widow lays this Foundation Stone.
In faith and hope. 29th May 1866.

Curiously, the stone was not laid where it can be seen – indeed there is no sign of it; all we know is that it was at the east end of the building. Since construction work only started a few weeks previously, it is likely that the stone was laid in the foundations which form the vault.

As a mark of gratitude for the building, the villagers presented an Illuminated Address to the Everett family signed by 179 members of the community.

The text reads:

Church of St John the Evangelist
Sutton Veny
1866

We the undersigned, the Rector, the Churchwardens and the Parishioners of the parish of Sutton Veny desire to express to Mrs Everett to Lieutenant Colonel Everett and the other

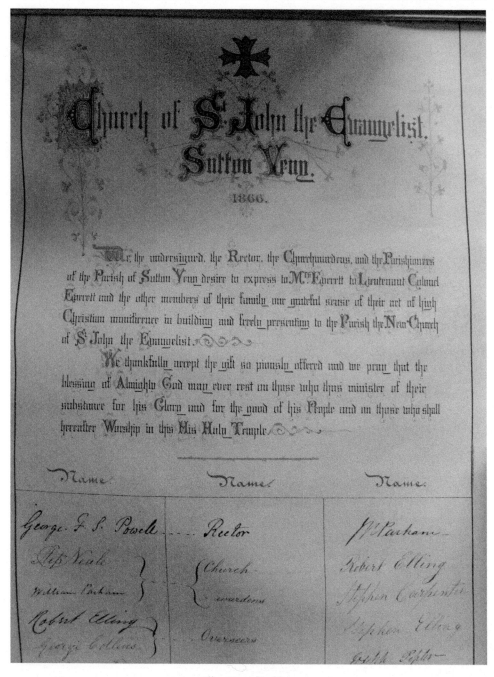

Illuminated address

members of their family our grateful sense of their act of high Christian Munificence in the
building and freely presenting to the Parish the New Church of St John the Evangelist.

We gratefully accept the gift so piously offered and we pray that the blessing of Almighty God may ever rest on those who thus minister of their substance for his Glory and for the good of his People and on those who shall hereafter Worship in this His Holy Temple.

Construction

THE BUILDERS WERE Rogers and Booth of Gosport, and given the completion timescale there could have been as many as 150 – 200 workers employed on the project at any one time. Casual labourers and a few craftsmen would have been drawn from nearby villages but the majority would have had to be brought in from miles away and these would all need to have been accommodated.

The principal building materials were sourced from a wide area. At Heytesbury and Warminster railway stations, two and three miles away respectively, there would have been a constant flow of horse-drawn carts to the present Alexander Field and the Everett's land on the opposite side of the High Street. In any event, stone and timber would have been rough cut by steam power and finished by craftsman, carefully co-ordinated by the Clerk of Works, Mr A Harrison (who declared in his application for the job that he 'did not drink').

Completion of the work was fixed for December 1867 just over 18 months away. As a result, the pace of building would have been unrelenting. In fact, and not unsurprisingly, the contract overran by almost six months.

Except for an enlarged vestry being added at the end of the century, the outward appearance of the building has remained unchanged.

The interior of the building was lit by oil lamps suspended from the arches of the nave. The fitting-out of the church involved considerable expense and it was here where villagers and other donors, having overcome their initial reservations about abandoning St Leonard's, could demonstrate their approval of their new church. Some contributed cash and others something more tangible – the altar, reredos, font, and the carved eagle lectern that had been exhibited at the second Great Exhibition in 1862. A number of pieces were identified with a memorial plaque. Some stained glass windows were completed at the time but some were added later over a period of years, each reflecting Old and New Testament parables and themes.

> **Initially the church was lit with hanging oil lamps and the verger used to watch the choir boys as they made their way through the vestry, otherwise one of them, usually an angelic looking one, used to flick spit with his fingers which caused the lamps' chimneys to explode if their aim was good.**

The consecration

IN CONTRAST TO the foundation stone ceremony, the consecration communion service was a high profile event. The 22nd April 1868 edition of the Wiltshire County Mirror gives an account of the service itself and the celebration banquet afterwards: *Such a number of carriages was probably never seen before on any one occasion in Sutton and the parish generally was a scene of great animation throughout the day.*[15]

Although it was reported that the church had a capacity of 400, it seems that upwards of 800 tickets had been applied for and issued, with extra chairs being placed in the nave and other parts of the church. It is difficult to imagine how so many could have been accommodated or how they could have seen proceedings because of the obstructing pillars, pulpit and lectern. At the time, these had become the most prominent features in the church, facing as many people as possible on the principle that hearing The Word was more important than seeing the actions of the celebrant at the altar and in the chancel.

The Bishop of Salisbury had been taken ill so at short notice the Bishop of Sodor and Man, who happened to be staying in Bournemouth, took his place. The Bishop of Salisbury was not the only one to be indisposed – the Rector George Powell had a severe cold and had lost his voice, so was unable to take part in the service.

The sermon was given by Rev. C. F. Hyde, of Dilton Marsh, who explained that his first impulse was to refuse the summons from his bishop but *then he knew that such a course would have the appearance of moral cowardice; besides which he felt confident that great allowances would be made, and by none more liberally than by his reverend brethren to whom he was called upon to preach.* He had, he said, been working on the sermon until 4 o'clock that morning.

With the service finished, the clergy and others formed a procession to accompany the Bishop as he consecrated the churchyard.

Afterwards the proceedings moved to the grounds of Greenhill where *in every respect, thoroughly genuine and English in its character, the hospitable doors of the mansion were not only thrown open to all comers, but a marquee, in which refreshments were provided on a most liberal scale for upwards of 600 guests. Afterwards a letter of good wishes from the Bishop of Salisbury was read out and there were a number of speeches inter-dispersed with* 'applause', 'laughter', 'hear, hear', and at the end, 'long and protracted cheering'.

> When the spire was built, it was topped with a cockerel weathervane 200 ft. above the ground. By 1886 it had become corroded and was brought down for repair and re-gilding. The work was never done

The church bells

T HE SIX BELLS which originally hung at St Leonard's were installed at St John's in 1868. It is one of 10 churches in the present Wylye Valley Team of which only four (Sutton Veny, Heytesbury, Boyton and Codford) still have active pealing bells. They each weigh between four and eight hundredweight (0.2 and 0.4 tonnes).

Church bells

The organ

T HE ORGAN WAS BUILT for the church in 1868 by the London firm of Gray & Davison, and is in a loft at the north side of the chancel. The cost was £464 2s 2d.[16] The case, with its spectacular array of decorated speaking pipes, is listed Grade 1 by the British Institute of Organ Studies as being of importance to the national heritage and deserving careful preservation.

The console is placed out of sight at the head of the north aisle, some 14 feet below the organ. The considerable distance between the two presented a challenge for the technology of the day, which employed a system of rods and levers known as tracker

A few of the 1,155 pipes

The organ console exposed

action; because the route of the mechanism is long and complex, the instrument is unusually heavy to play.

The main structure of the organ is original, but some alterations have been made. Not all the stops were inserted in 1868; vacant spaces were filled in 1971 by Peter Hutchins of Coleford, who also re-arranged some of the existing pipework, thus perceptibly altering the organ's character. Nevertheless, the sound is rewarding and commands the church admirably.

Robin Winn of Melksham overhauled the organ in 1985; John Budgen of Crockerton carried out some restoration and improvement work in 2003. The organ now has two manuals, 20 stops, and 1,155 pipes of which only some are shown here.

Incidentally, the neighbouring church of St Cosmas and St Damian, Sherrington, has a small organ built by the same builder in the same period.

No mention should be made of Sutton Veny's instrument without referring to Oliver Lines (1895–1967). The Lines family ran the bakery and shop 'Fairview' in the High Street. He started as St John's organist at the age of 12 and played for 60 years until he died from a stroke after slipping down in the snow on his way to church. He had never missed a Sunday except during the time he served in the 1914-18 War.[17]

Oliver Lines

The churchyard

A S THE BISHOP'S PROCESSION wound its way, consecrating the churchyard that day in 1868, no one would have imagined that in a mere 47 years, a corner where they were walking would be completely filled, and one day be known by a name not yet even perceived – a Commonwealth War Graves Cemetery.

The first soldier to be buried there was Corporal Joseph Clements, a British soldier, in September 1915. The first ANZAC soldier was an Australian, Gunner Albert Hodge, in October 1916.[18]

The Australian Cross of Sacrifice was erected in the 1920s with wooden Allied crosses progressively replaced with Portland stone. In about 1963 this part of the graveyard became the responsibility of the Commonwealth War Graves Commission.

In addition to the allied soldiers, 38 German prisoners of war also died at the Sutton Veny Military Hospital. Whilst some villages in the country refused to allow the remains of the enemy to be buried within their community, Sutton Veny had no such compunction and 38 were given a Christian burial, although with no firing party or military honours. Some were interred three or four to a grave. They lay roughly near where the Cross of Sacrifice now stands.

German war graves

In 1963, as part of a national initiative, their remains were exhumed and relocated to the German Military Cemetery at Cannock Chase, Staffordshire.

In about 1960 the then Rector Donovan Evening (Rector 1958–1963) suggested that a memorial chapel be dedicated in St John's to the memory of the ANZAC soldiers and nurses. This is in the south transept and the national flags of Australia and of New Zealand hang either side of the altar with a Roll of Honour displayed next to them.

The graves of the soldiers resulted in the churchyard filling sooner than had been anticipated, and by 1999 it became necessary to create an extension from a corner of the adjacent Alexander Memorial Field. This was consecrated in 2001.

In 2014, St John's registered with the Wiltshire Living Churchyards & Cemeteries Project, which encourages the conservation of the churchyard's flora and fauna. This has been particularly successful in an area to the south of the church, which is left unmown from April to July in order to encourage the growth of wild flowers and grasses. A mown labyrinth has been created in the churchyard extension for interest.

Rectors of Sutton Veny from 1297

1297 John de Bradeham
1304 John le Breton
1309 John Enebury
1309 Richard de Berton
1336 William de Abingdon
1339 Henry Palgrove
1360 William de Boulton
1361 Nicholas Poywick
1376 John Stretton
1398 Robert Elande
1417 Simon Sydenham
1421 Thomas Sircestre
1453 Thomas Preay
14 -- John Ayssh
1502 Thomas Benet
1507 Henry Mompesson
1509 Cuthbert Tunstall
1516 John Poote
15 -- John Long
1582 Thomas Dobbes
1597 Thomas Hide
1618 Walter Coningsby DD
1635 Henry Swaddon
1646 Daniel Burgess
1660   –
1670 John Cleavely
1680 Richard Bayly MA
1716 Francis Holland

1731 Edward Taylor MA
1764 Joseph Pain
1766 William Davison
1780 Brounker Thring DD
1812 William D Thring DD
1854 George F S Powell
1888 Arthur W Booker
1896 Arthur J Everett MA
1907 Arthur Sewell MA
1923 Eustace A Chorley MA
1946 Howard M Bennett MA
1958 Donovan V Evening
1963 Edward Wade-Stubbs LthBA
1967 Roland C Desch MBE AKC
1971 John Rhys-Hughes BA
Priest in Charge
1975   John Rhys-Hughes BA

Rector amalgamated the Parish of Sutton
Veny, Heytesbury, Norton Bavant, Knook
& Tytherington in 1977

1981 Peter R. English
1991 Robert R. Webb MA
Upper Wylye Valley Team
1997   Hugh Hoskins
2004   John H. Tomlinson BSc
2016   Alison Morley

Baptist Chapel Sutton End

BAPTIST CHAPEL SUTTON END

THIS BUILDING WAS in Sutton Veny parish until a boundary adjustment in 1934; it is now in the parish of Longbridge Deverill.

There are unverified suggestions that the formation of the congregation may have been influenced by the spread of nonconformity by Scottish stonemasons rebuilding Longleat House. However, their first record is in 1669 when it was *admonished for erring in its ways*.

This is one of the earliest nonconformist chapels in the area and was built in 1739 on 'The Waste' at the corner of Five Ash Lane and today's A350. The present chapel was built in about 1777 with the first recorded minister being John Clark in 1798 (who walked the eight miles there and back from Frome every Sunday to conduct services). He died aged 92.

It ceased to be used for worship in 1980 although the original pews and pulpit remain in place.

Congregational Church

THE CONGREGATIONAL CHURCH

BY THE LATTER PART of the 17th century, religious turbulence had settled somewhat. Protestant Christians who did not conform to the governance of the established Church of England were permitted, under licence, to set up and worship in their own independent churches.

The records of the congregation are contained in The Church Book[19] and give an account of the formation and activity.

In Warminster a church was set up in Common Close (now The Close). Ministers from the town visited neighbouring villages and in 1679 there is a record of Thomas Gibbons preaching to a group of Independents at an unidentified house in Sutton Veny. The group continued and expanded as further licences were issued for meetings at other houses.

As the group expanded, it was clear that they needed a permanent meeting house, and in 1793 a new chapel was built on land forming part of the garden of Edward Imber in the High Street.

Initially pastors came from Warminster and other nearby churches. Later permanent appointments were made with the incumbent living in The Manse, which was a short distance up the High Street. By 1801, the average attendance on a Sunday morning was 116 with in the afternoon 151, and in the evening, 300; the village population at the time was roughly 850.

In 1811 John Butcher became the pastor. The Church Book describes how,

Mr. Butcher continued to labour among them with considerable success till the spring of the year 1816. At which time the Typhus fever prevailed in the parish and in the family of Mr. Butcher. At length the dire disorder attacked the father as well as the children – He languished more than a month when he breathed his last on the last day of May 1816 – leaving behind, to lament his loss, a widow, seven small children and an affectionate people...

In 1855 it was decided that a new church was needed. The practical solution was to buy land adjoining the burial ground. It was to have 250 sittings and be designed in the Norman style.

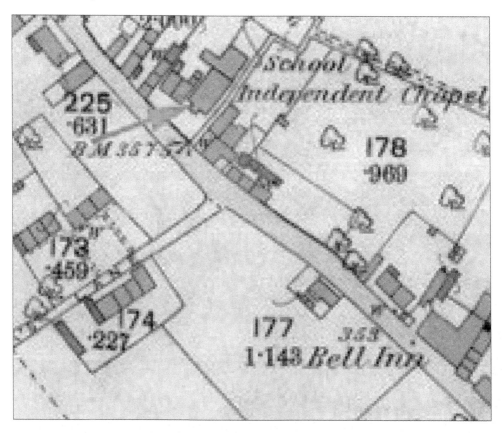

Ordnance Survey 1886

The building of the chapel did not have wholehearted approval in the village; in one instance a farmer threatened to pull down the walls as it was being built. It's not known if it was vandalised but it was indeed completed and at the Dedication Service on 11 June 1856,

' *...hymns were sung, printed for the occasion. A large tent was provided for the Dinner and Tea, and for the Evening Service, at which 600 persons attended.*'

The lectern

The Church adopted a set of rules by which members were expected to comply. One of them related to alcohol, *the fruit of drunkenness and worldliness – warning others that they should take warning and live nearer to the Lord.* The penalty for this transgression was suspension, or in extreme repetition, expulsion. There was an example in 1876 with the case of Betsy Oliver and George Cooper who '*were brought before the Meeting, and with sorrow and regret the friends present felt it their duty to suspend them for want of a Godly sorrow and contrition for their past inconsistencies.*'

The Church Book gives no further detail and it can only speculate how the congregation fared over the following hundred years. But it will no doubt have continued to offer spiritual guidance and support to its members and will have had some influence in the life of the village during the two world wars that were to follow.

Fredrick Varnon. Pastor 1897-1941 outside the Manse

There is an interesting insight into the life of the church during the Pastorship of Wilfred Davis in 1943. He wrote that there was only one service held on a Sunday evening and no meetings at all during the week. The demands of the War Effort took their toll for *there was no choir, no communion services, no nothing.* He does go on to say however, how the Parade Service for troops from the [Deverill Road] camp gave him *much encouragement.*

Elsewhere he describes the graveyard and playground at the back of the church *as being in a disgraceful condition – weeds and thistles were five feet high.* There were no records naming the occupants of the graves, so he had to do the best he could by enquiring who wanted their monuments left as they were. No one seemed interested, so he levelled those that were nameless and cleared away the weeds. He remarked that he had plenty of advice and commendation about what he was doing, but no one offered to help.

Eight years later, with the departure of a later pastor, Mr Jenkins, in 1951, the Independent churches of Codford, Wylye, Heytesbury and Sutton Veny amalgamated under the control of Codford. By 1962, the membership of the congregation was only eight and there was no resident minister. The church is believed to have closed in the mid-1960s and had been demolished by 1970, when the land was sold and the former school attached to it. The history of the house is outlined in chapter 10 of this book, A Stroll around the Village – Little Hall.

The graveyard is now a conservation area and maintained by the Parish Council.

The Pastors of Sutton Veny Congregational Church.[19]

(Some dates are uncertain)

1793	Mr E.D. Jackson	1842 – 1894	No details
1794 – 1799	Itinerant Pastors in rotation	1895 – 1896	Frederick Longman
1800	Mr Holloway	1897 – 1941	Fredrick Varnon
1801	Mr Butcher	1942 – 1945	Wilfred Davis
1802 – 1805	Mr Vardy	1946 – 1947	None
1806 – 1815	Itinerant pastors	1947 – 1951	W.J. Jenkins
1816 – 1841	Mr Scammell	1951 – 195?	Alfred Shave

THE MISSION HALL

THE MISSION HALL stood adjacent to 103-105 High Street. It is not known for sure how long the corrugated iron building was in use, but probably between 1890 and about 1930. Meetings were held by visiting evangelical missions and were popular events.

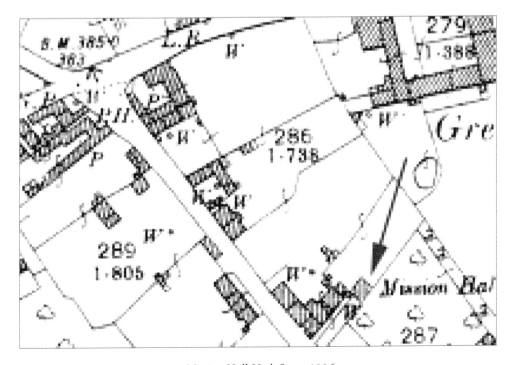

Mission Hall High Street 1886

PRIMITIVE METHODIST CHAPEL, SUTTON PARVA

T HE PRIMITIVE METHODIST CHURCH is a 'body of holiness' within the
Methodist tradition. Nothing is known about the building but the 1867 OS map
clearly shows where it stood. Worship is believed to have ceased in about 1933.

The building was subsequently used as a dwelling and called Chapel House
during the Second World War and for about 10 years afterwards. It was disused for a
long time and, with the nearby derelict cottages having been pulled down, the present
houses (1 and 2 New Cottages) were built on the site in 1959.

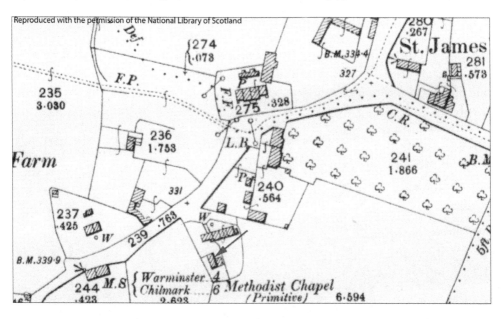

Primitive Methodist Chapel 1899, Sutton Parva

5
PRIMARY SCHOOL

WHAT IS BELIEVED to be the first school in the village was in Duck Street and it is described in chapter 10, A Stroll around the Village – The Old School House.

Some of the material about the primary school is taken from *Sutton Veny C. E. School 1850–1950*, published in 1988 with the kind permission of its author David Chatterton who was headmaster for 19 years from 1968.

With the 1870 Education Act came a growing compulsion that all children between the ages of 5 and 13 went to school. With this it quickly became apparent that the building in Duck Street was inadequate and that a larger building was needed.

The site chosen was on land next to the recently built church of St John the Evangelist. The designer is not known but it was built in the Ecclesiastical Gothic style that was favoured for church schools at the time. Using some stone from the old church of St Leonard's, the building consisted of a large room which was about 44 feet x 21 feet, with a small classroom adjoining.

Mrs John Everett laid the foundation stone of the new school on 10 April 1872. The inscription read:

To the glory of God
And for the education of the youth of this Parish
In the principles of the Church of England

Curiously, as with St. John's Church the stone cannot be seen; it is assumed that it too was laid in the foundations.

The Rector Powell wrote about the occasion:

'The service used was Bishop Hamilton's. Miss Everett played the harmonium and the children and choir sang... the school children had each a bun and two oranges; Mrs Everett gave the bun and we the oranges. The party retired to the Rectory for luncheon. We sat some 31. The workmen also had something. Fine Day — most satisfactory. Laus Deo.'

The report in the Warminster Herald on 15 April 1873 gives a glimpse of the sense of pride and anticipation the new building gave the children, their parents and the community:

' *...the new school room in this parish was formally opened in the presence of a large number of friends and parishioners. The doors were then opened and the large and lofty school-room was filled from end to end. The service was commenced by the Rector, the choir and the school children making the responses. The Rev Arthur Everett declared the school opened for the purpose for which it had been erected, namely that every child in the parish might have the opportunity of receiving a useful and religious education and that based upon the distinct principles of the Church of England. . . After a few words from the Rector, the National Anthem was sung and the party separated — the children to enjoy an afternoon's holiday and a little festival which the kindness of Mrs Everett had provided.*'

The clock tower and bell

THE CLOCK TOWER was paid for by Ellen Wansey in memory of her husband Edward. In the *Buildings of England. Wiltshire 1975*, the writer Nicholaus Pevsner describes it as *'gruesome... an object lesson in the range of Victorian values'*.

The clock would have served a very useful purpose in a period when few of the population carried watches. The mechanism is quite large (about the size of a modern office desk) because it needs to be powerful enough to drive the hands. It was built by Thwaites and Reed of Brighton who, incidentally, also made and maintain the clocks of Westminster Abbey and Horse Guards. Interestingly, when the company was contacted as part of the research for this book, they mentioned that their records showed that it had not been serviced since 1911 – suggesting that perhaps another one might be due! The bell itself was made by Mears and Stainbank (now the Whitechapel Foundry) who also cast Big Ben, the USA Pennsylvania Liberty Bell and the Horse Guards bell.

School tower

The Parish Council took over the responsibility for the clock's maintenance in 1936. During the war it stopped striking and no one could be found to mend it. The striking mechanism was subsequently detached from the clock and the two remained separated. Instead, that bell announcing school occurrences was rung by hand. It was heavy and difficult to get swinging properly.

In 1953 the clock stopped because the vertical wooden ladder up to the clock chamber had become unsafe and it could no longer be wound. It was to remain still for the next 56 years.

The clock and bell

It was David Chatterton who suggested the clock should be set going again, but it would be years before enough money could be found to pay for it. With fundraising and contributions from the Parish Council and the Flower Show, the repair was started. A team dismantled it piece by piece, each to be cleaned and sent away for repair and restoration. A recycled metal water tower ladder replaced the wooden one and the clock was reinstalled with an electric winding mechanism. As a final touch, the clock faces were re-gilded with gold leaf. Since there was no longer any need to have a bell to assemble the children to their classes, it was decided that it should be connected to the clock instead. Villagers were invited to vote on the hours it should chime; virtually everyone agreed that it should be between 7am and 10pm. In May 2009 the Warminster Journal reported *the chiming of the bell by itself for the first time was celebrated with children maypole dancing and singing.*

The standard of teaching

THE DIOCESAN INSPECTOR'S REPORT about the standard of religious instruction was on the whole complimentary. In 1876 for instance, when Mr Horwood was the headmaster with 51 pupils, the inspector wrote:

The tone of the school is good and the instruction has been carefully given. The infants should however, be more accurate in their repetition of the Lord's Prayer and Ten Commandments.

From 1873 to 1888 there seems to have been only the one mistress with a pupil-teacher to help take as many as five classes. In time, however, several more teachers joined the staff after a new extension in 1898. Whilst that eased the crowded conditions, numbers continued to rise.

Paper was still scarce and expensive at this time so the children were using slates made from a piece of quarry slate set in a wooden frame. They did not use chalk, but a slate stylus (called a pencil). Children had to bring a dampened cloth or sponge so that they could clean the slate surface and start again; often they would just use their own spit and the cuff of their sleeve. It is believed that this process is the origin of the phrase 'to wipe the slate clean'. The pencil was generally sharpened on the stonework of the wall and signs of this can still be seen today in the small courtyard at the entrance.

Stylus pencil sharpening marks

In her memoirs, Gertrude McCracken (b.1907) recalls:[3]

The school consisted of one long room running the whole length of the building, the Juniors' class and the Babies' rooms housing the 3 to 5 or 6 year olds. The Babies were taught as I recall later on by a Mrs. Poore who came as a junior teacher from the Congregation Chapel school when it closed about 1908. The walls of the Babies' class had a drawing board around for the children to draw on. They wrote on slates. They also had large trays of sand, a big rocking horse for the children's

amusement and a big doll's house with real furniture. Only the good children were allowed to play with that, but I am afraid that much as I yearned and prayed for it, I never achieved that distinction. The large room was divided by manoeuvrable screens, brown canvas, unusually drab!

On entering school at 9 a.m. we all trooped into the large room to sing the morning hymn and gabble the morning

prayer. After roll-call, we all marched to our respective places to start the lessons. At that time the seating was long backless forms and two-tiered desks to match, very hard on the back. Sometime after, the school was given an uplift. The dark brown paint was changed to dark green on the lower half of the walls and light green above. The long benches disappeared and we had small desks each to seat two children. The heating came from two tall, round iron stoves in the large room and an open fire in the Babies' room.

Because of the shortage of food during the First World War, the Board of Education allowed children to be excused attendance for a limited period to assist in agricultural work. A number of 12 or 13 year olds did in fact leave for this purpose.

One of the problems experienced by the teachers between the wars, was how to cope with the very wide age range of 3 to 13, particularly when it came to catering for the needs of the older children. In 1931 Sutton Veny ceased to be an all-age school with pupils leaving at 14. Instead it became a Junior and Infant School catering for children up to 11 years of age, with education for younger children being called 'Primary' and above that age, 'Secondary'. At this point there were 70 children on roll and three members of staff, but in that year those above 11 were transferred to the Avenue School in Warminster.

This exodus of the older pupils meant that in the 1930s the headteacher had fewer and younger children to deal with, making it easier to engage in more practical and active learning. There were field trips and visits and, judging from the reports of inspectors, this gradual move from the rigid, formal way of learning to the inclusion of activity and experience was very successful. The HMI report of February 1937 reported that, *The children are receiving a balanced and varied training which results in their being well-mannered, alert, responsive and interested in their lessons.*

The Second World War saw another change affecting the life of the school, when 14 evacuees arrived from London. It is unclear how these extra children were accommodated or their ages or sex, but by the following May there were only five evacuees remaining. It is also unclear why the others had returned home to re-join their families, but later the school was to admit 15 further evacuees together with their teacher from Beckford School, West Hampstead. A former resident of the village remembers their teacher being fed up with country life and asking to go back to London.

Evacuees seem to have continued to come and go fairly regularly during the war years and in 1945, there were six remaining. In all it seems that whilst their presence made things difficult for the teachers, the children settled down quite happily and felt at home.

Apart from the evacuees, the war did not seem to affect the life of the school very much, though the children were issued with gas masks. The arrival of American GIs at the camp on the Deverill Road made an interesting diversion for the pupils.

The 1944 Education Act had a profound influence in England and Wales. Sutton Veny school had to decide to choose to take either a Controlled or Aided status. The preference was to be Controlled by the Local Education Authority. Accordingly they became responsible for the appointment of the teachers and the expenses of the school. Religious instruction was to be in accordance with an agreed syllabus, but parents had the right to opt in, or opt out of denominational teaching. One-third of the managers were to be appointed by the Church and two-thirds by the Authority.

Another change brought about by the same Act was the Eleven-Plus exam, which determined which school each child should go on to for their secondary education. The numbers staying for lunch grew to such an extent that the children had to eat at their desks, covered by a plastic mat. This was not very satisfactory, as food sometimes spilled over onto the floor or into the ink-well.

Whilst the general ethos of the school remains essentially the same, the complexities of life in the twenty-first century have inevitably brought a number of significant changes as to how it is run. In the 21st century the numbers of pupils had reached 170, with many coming from outside the Parish.

The ANZAC posy tradition

FRED JUDD (B.1911), whose father was the landlord of The Bell, remembered how the posy tradition began.

> In 1916, *Me and three other village children, Dennis Cundick, Vera Gough and Phyllis Poore, had been up Five Ash Lane where primroses grew. We picked bunches and bunches and brought them back to the village.* Wondering what to do with them, Phyllis's mother (Elsie Poore, the Infant teacher who had come from the Congregation Chapel school after it had closed), suggested '*why don't you put them on the poor soldiers graves.*' So that is what they did.

Whilst this was a simple and spontaneous gesture, it so impressed the Rector, Arthur Sewell, that he held a School Commemoration Service the following year with the pupils laying posies on the grave of each soldier. As far as is known, it has been repeated by the children in one form or another, almost every ANZAC Day since.

The posy service has been broadcast several times on Australian radio and referred to on TV news. Over the years the Australian connection has deepened with substantial numbers of family history enquiries being made to the school and a gentle trickle visiting the graves. On one special occasion in 1980 an ANZAC veteran, Bob Hocking (83), visited the school to thank the children for these tokens of remembrance. While being taken round the ANZAC graves, he remarked that he knew some of the soldiers buried there.

Mrs Elsie Poore, Mr JW Carr (headteacher) and some pupils circa 1919

Childrens' ANZAC Centenary Service 2015

There is a postscript to this story. Elsie Poore died in 1968 and lies buried in the churchyard, against the school playground wall only a dozen yards from the war graves. In April 2016, the centenary of the first posy occasion, the headteacher Rachael Brotherton, laid a posy on her grave in remembrance of Elsie and of all the teachers who have taught children in the village over the years.

Headteacher Rachael Brotherton at the grave of Elsie Poore. Posy anniversary 2016

The childrens' posies incorporate flowers donated by their families and include laurel to represent honour, rosemary for remembrance and from the Geraldton Western Australia Returned and Services League, poppies as a memorial to the fallen. As the headteacher said in 2016,

> *Each child lays a posy on one of the war graves to pay respect to those soldiers and nurses who bravely gave their lives and who are laid to rest here next to the school in our community but so far away from their own homes and family. This loving act has a profound impact on their empathy and cultural understanding. It is a very moving service.*

The school classes are named after towns and cities in Australia and New Zealand to reflect and recognise their commitment to the ANZAC link. The class with the youngest children is Auckland and moving up through the school to the next class, to Brisbane, Canberra, Darwin, Elliston, Geraldton and Nelson. Their participation in the ceremony fosters the relationship between them and our society and with it, strong links have developed with schools in New Zealand and Australia. Visitors and relatives of those who died frequently contact or visit Sutton Veny to share memories and exchange information and an expanding range of resources.

Headteachers

Mrs. E.Long	1850s	Mr. J.W.Carr	1919-1929
Miss R.Blake	1850s	Mrs. F.Lister	1929-1943
Miss C. Mead	1860s	Miss K. Parkin	1943-1947
Miss E.Pierce	1870s	Miss O. D. Balance	1947-1952
Miss C. Everley	1880s	Mrs. Gwen Lewis	1952-1968
Mr. C.J.Edwood	1880s-90s	Mr. David Chatterton	1968-1987
Mr. E. C.Morgan	1895-1903	Mrs. Christine Folker	1987-2008
Mr. G.E.Wilkins	1903-1911	Miss Rachael Brotherton	2008-
Mr. J. S.D.Thomas	1912-1918		

6

SOCIAL AND ECONOMIC

THE POPULATION OF SUTTON VENY

A T THE TIME of the Domesday Book (1086) the Sutton manor was divided between three land owners with a population of 160 to 200. This did not include Newnham. At the beginning of the 17th century it is believed the population was about 360.[20]

The earliest surviving records of births and burials date from the 1570s[21] when, although numbers subsequently fluctuate over the decades, births regularly exceeded burials so that by the first formal count in 1801 the population was 622. It peaked in 1871 when 1,881 people lived in the village.

It is interesting to compare the numbers against Heytesbury and Codford over the same period.[22]

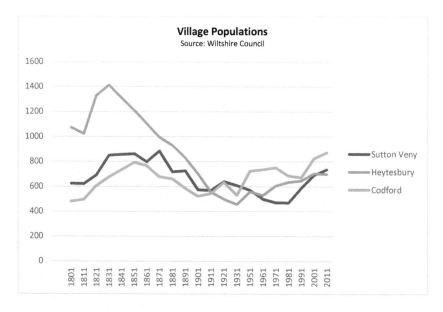

Village populations 1801–2011

EMPLOYMENT

Industry

THE MOST SIGNIFICANT area of employment in the parish was generated by the agricultural industry. This encompassed not only the production of crops, livestock, wool and timber but also the ancillary trades of wagon transport, blacksmith, wheelwright, milling and timber. In addition, the land in this part of the South West had a reputation for producing some of the best malting barley in the country.

Wiltshire and Somerset had been associated with the production of wool and cloth since the 15th and 16th Centuries. South of the village, the Downs were perfect for grazing sheep, but from the 19th century, increasing wool imports reduced prices to such a degree, that local producers began to be squeezed out of the market.

Nevertheless, local wool continued to be favoured because of the quality and quantity of the fleece used in the production of Melton cloth with its tough, dense and pliable finish popular for clothing and uniforms. As a consequence, there had been something of a short-term recovery during both the Napoleonic wars.

Prior to being sold on to clothiers, bales of raw fleeces were sorted and stored in sheds and barns; the merchant handling this product was a wool stapler. There were several such merchants in the region but in Sutton Veny the most prosperous was the Elling family. The fourth generation of which was Robert (1827–1916) who, in about 1850, built a multi-storey woolstore in the courtyard beside his house, The Knapp in the High Street.

Over time, with the demand for wool continuing to decline, and with the increase in the demand for food, the Downs were converted to arable production. By the beginning of the Second World War they had all largely been ploughed up.

Mills

WHILST NOT POWERFUL enough to drive heavy industry, the upper reaches of the Wylye river were adequate to drive the handful of water mills built on its banks as the flow threaded its way around the top of the parish. The two principal processes for mills in the parish were fulling (the finishing processes in the manufacture of cloth) and grist (grinding corn).

Bull Mill in Crockerton handled a different process – silk. Whilst not in Sutton Veny parish, this mill was a substantial complex of buildings. Until its closure in the mid 19th century was a significant employer, attracting workers from a wide area including Newnham.

Jobs Mill 1910

A short distance upstream on the west side of the parish at the bottom of Five Ash Lane is Sutton Veny Mill. This was a grist mill, later to be called Jobs Mill after a father and son partnership in the 19th century. It closed down in the early 20th century and subsequently became a private house.

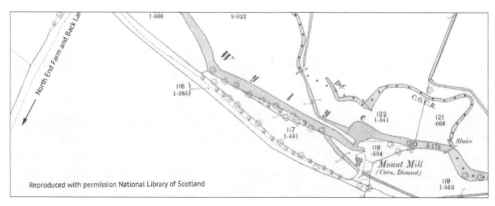

Reproduced with permission National Library of Scotland

Mount Mill 1884

At the north eastern corner of the parish was Mount Mill. The original building dated back to at least 1541 and, over time, had been both a fulling and a grist mill. It was advertised for sale in the 1760s, described as having a *good house and trout fishery with two fulling stocks with room to work a third.* The Haines family is believed to been the last to live there in 1866. It was demolished sometime afterwards and the site is now largely obscured by woodland.

TRADES AND OCCUPATIONS

THE 1848 AND the 1939 editions of Kelly's Directories, a Victorian version of today's Yellow Pages, and a summary of the census returns 1841-1911, give an overview of the trades in the parish.

Trade	1849	1855	1859	1867	1880	1895	1903	1907	1911	1915	1920	1927
Baker						2	3	2	2	2		1
Banks										3		
Beer Retailer						2	1	1	1	1	1	1
Benefit Society						1	2	2	2	2	1	1
Blacksmith	1	1	2	2	2	2	1	1	1			1
Carpenter	2	1	1	1	1	2	2	1	1	1	1	1
Carrier			1	1		3	2	1	2	1	1	
Cinema										1		
Coal Merchant						1	1	1	1	1	1	
Draper										1		
Fire Loss Assessor						1	1	1				
Grocer							2	2	2	2	2	2
Inn Keeper	2	2	2	2	2	2	2	2	2	2	2	2
Laundry						1	1	1	1	1		1
Miller	1	1	1	1	1	1	1					
Plumber							1	1		1		1
Post Office	1	1	1	1	1	1	1	1	1	1	1	1
Racehorse Trainer												1
Refreshment Rooms							1				2	1
Registrar				1								

Trades in Sutton Veny 1849–1927

More often than not, there are discrepancies in the detail when comparing occupations in census and other sources. For example, the head of a household may describe himself as having one occupation when speaking with the Kelly representative (who was very often a clergyman or other upright member of the community), but another when talking to the census numerator (who themselves will make generalisations for the sake of uniformity or simplicity).

OCCUPATIONS 1841 – 1911
Ancestry ©

Community

1841		1851		1861		1871		1881		1891		1901		1911	
Clergyman	1	Clergyman	1	Police	1	Clergyman	1	Clergyman	1	Clerical	4	Clergyman	2	Clergyman	1
Police	1	Police	1	School Assist	4	Police	1	Police Consta	1	Police Consta	1	Postman	1	School other	1
Watchman	4	School Teach	2		5			School Assist	1	School Assist	2	Postmaster	1	School Teach	3
	6		4					School other	1	School Teach	3	School Assist	2		5
								School Teach	3		10	School Teach	4		
									7				11		

Domestic

1841		1851		1861		1871		1881		1891		1901		1911	
Gardener	4	Coachman	2	Cook	2	Coachman	2	Coachman	2	Coachman	2	Butler	1	Butler	2
Groom	2	Gardener	7	Gardener	3	Gardener	7	Cook	2	Cook	3	Cook	1	Coach/Chauf	4
Nurse	1	Governess	1	Groom	3	Governess	1	Gardener	5	Gardener	7	Gardener	11	Drink Inn/Sal	4
Service F	36	Groom	1	Housekeeper	2	Groom	3	Groom	2	Groom	2	Governess	1	Gardener	13
Service M	14	Housekeeper	1	Nurse	1	Nursemaid	5	Nurse	1	Housekeeper	2	Groom	8	Groom	5
	57	Service F	27	Service F	27	Service F	20	Service F	15	Service F	3	Housekeeper	3	Nurse Medic	1
		Service M	6	Service M	3	Service M	17	Service M	1	Service M	8	Nurse	1	Service F	24
			45		41		55		28		28	Nurse Medic	1	Service F	10
												Service M	6		63
												Service F	11		
													44		

Leisure

1841		1851		1861		1871		1881		1891		1901		1911	
Inn/Sales	3	Hunt Groom	3	Brewer	1	Hunt Groom	5	Hunt Groom	10	Hunt Groom	12	Hunt Groom	3	Hunt Groom	2
	3	Hunt Servant	1	Hunt Groom	5	Hunt Kennel	2	Hunt Kennel	1	Inn/Sales	1	Hunt Kennel	1	Hunt Kennel	1
		Inn/Sales	2	Inn/Sales	2	Huntsman	1	Hunt Servant	1	Inn/Sales	5	Hunt Servant	2	Hunt Servant	8
			6		8	Inn/Sales	3	Huntsman	4		18	Huntsman	1	Inn/Sales	2
							11	Inn/Sales	6			Inn/Sales	2		13
									22				9		

Land

1841		1851		1861		1871		1881		1891		1901		1911	
Bailiff	2	Dairy	1	Bailiff	1	Bailiff	1	Bailiff	2	Bailiff	2	Farmer	10	Bailiff	1
Farmer	6	Farmer	10	Farmer	30	Dairy	4	Farmer	8	Dairy	2	Livestock	7	Farmer	14
Gamekeeper	4	Shepherd	5	Gamekeeper	15	Farmer	5	Gamekeeper	1	Farmer	6	Market Gdner	1	Gamekeeper	1
Shepherd	2	Wagoner	7	Hedging	1	Gamekeeper	1	Shepherd	8	Gamekeeper	1	Shepherd	6	Livestock	7
Worker	157	Woodman	2	Herdsman	4	Market Garde	8	Wagoner	2	Shepherd	8	Wagoner	11	Shepherd	6
Yeoman	5	Worker	165	Market Gdner	1	Shepherd	13	Woodman	1	Wagoner	1	Worker	22	Wagoner	16
	176		190	Shepherd	11	Wagoner	4	Worker	63	Wood Worke	2		57	Woodman	1
				Wagoner	9	Woodman	1		85	Worker	103			Worker	55
				Woodman	3	Worker	117			Yeoman	2				101
				Worker	90	Yeoman	1				127				
				Yeoman	1		155								
					166										

Manufacture

1841		1851		1861		1871		1881		1891		1901		1911	
Fuller	1	Nailor	1	Silk factory	4	Silk factory	10	Silk factory	8	Silk factory	3	Wool Sorter	4	Wool Sorter	1
Miller	2	Silk factory	1	Weaver	2	Wool Sorter	3	Weaver	1	Soap maker	1	Wool Stapel	1	Wool Stapel	2
Tanner	1	Tanner	1	Wool Sorter	8	Wool Stapel	6	Wool Sorter	9	Wool Sorter	6		5		3
Weaver	1	Wool Sorter	5	Wool Stapel	1		19	Wool Stapel	2	Wool Stapel	1				
Wool Sorter	22	Wool Stapel	2		15				20		11				
Wool Stapel	4		10												
	31														

Retail

1841		1851		1861		1871		1881		1891		1901		1911	
Baker	3	Baker	2	Baker	2	Baker	3	Baker	1	Baker/Grocer	3	Bailiff	2	Baker	6
Butcher	1	Baker/Grocer	3	Baker/Grocer	1	Baker/Grocer	4	Baker/Grocer	2	Dressmaker	6	Baker	2	Baker/Grocer	4
Cordwainer	3	Cordwainer	1	Dressmaker	10	Cordwainer	3	Cordwainer	1	Fish Hawker	1	Dressmaker	1	Dressmaker	3
Grocer	2	Dressmaker	6	Ironmonger	1	Dressmaker	1	Dressmaker	2	Grocer	1	Grocer	2	Tailor	1
Harness Make	1	Shoemaker	4	Shoemaker	4	Peddler	1	Grocer	1	Shoemaker	1	Shopkeeper	1		14
Shoemaker	3	Tailor	3	Shopworker	2	Shoemaker	5	Shoemaker	3	Tailor	1	Tailor	1		
Tailor	8		19	Tailor	9	Tailor	1	Shopkeeper	2		13		10		
	21				28		21	Tailor	1						
									14						

Service

1841		1851		1861		1871		1881		1891		1901		1911	
Blacksmith	4	Blacksmith	1	Blacksmith	5	Blacksmith	5	Blacksmith	4	Blacksmith	4	Carpenter	3	Auctioneer	1
Carpenter	8	Carpenter	15	Builder	1	Carpenter	10	Carpenter	5	Builder	1	Clerical	1	Blacksmith	1
Coal Merchan	1	Carter	4	Carpenter	4	Clerical	1	Clerical	2	Butter Maker	1	Coachman	2	Carpenter	4
Dealer gen	1	Clerical	3	Carter	6	Coal Merchan	2	Haulier	10	Carpenter	3	Coal Merchan	2	Clerical	3
Handyman	1	Dealer Livesto	2	Coal Merchan	2	Compositor	1	Labourer Gen	30	Coal Merchan	3	Haulier	4	Coal Merchan	1
Labourer Gen	4	Laundry	4	Labourer Gen	5	Haulier	7	Laundry	2	Haulier	5	Labourer Gen	9	Dealer gen	1
Laundry	2	Mason	2	Laundry	1	Labourer Gen	7	Pond Maker	1	Labourer Gen	11	Laundry	6	Dealer Livesto	2
Painter	2	Quarryman	1	Mason	2	Laundry	9	Railway	1	Laundry	8	Plumber	2	Haulier	3
Plasterer	2	Scavenger	1	Midwife	1	Mason	5	Scavenger	1	Mason	1	Railway	2	Labourer Gen	8
Post	2	Thatcher	3	Miller	1	Miller	1	Thatcher	3	Miller	2	Roadmender	1	Laundry	7
Wheelright	3		36	Thatcher	3	Painter	2		64	Plumber	2	Sawyer	1	Mason	1
	31			Wheelwright	3	Pond Maker	1			Post	2	Thatcher	2	Miller	1
					42	Thatcher	1			Railway	1	Wheelwright	1	Post	3
						Wheelwright	5			Road contract	1		37	Railway	1
							58			Thatcher	3			Static engine	1
											48			Thatcher	1
															39

Other

1841		1851		1861		1871		1881		1891		1901		1911	
Pauper	3	Pauper	17	Pauper	0	Pauper	18	Pauper	13	Pauper	2	Pauper	0	Pauper	0
		Pauper Agric	38												
			55												

© Ancestry.Com

Occupation Summaries 1841–1911

The first census noting the occupations of individuals was taken in 1841, and indicates how villagers were earning their living. Whilst the area including Sutton Veny was reasonably consistent, there were, following parish boundary changes, minor variations at the periphery towards North Crockerton and towards Bishopstrow.

In this graph, an analyses has been prepared showing the occupations for the 300 or so workers (which included working children), separated into eight categories.

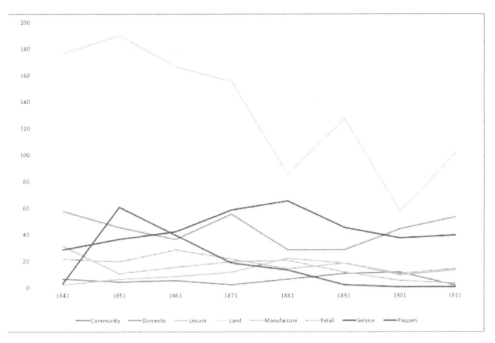

Occupation trends 1841–1911

A look at the numbers employed in Service gives something of an insight into the social structure of the village. In 1861, for example, the staff at Greenhill with Joseph and Frances Everett and their two unmarried adult daughters were a housekeeper, ladies maid, cook, house maid, kitchen maid, butler, coachman, footman. At the Rectory, the Rector George Powell, his wife and five small children made do with a governess and three domestic servants.

'Farming' was a wide description which encompassed owners and tenants with landholdings of all sizes across the parish. In the 1861 census for example, William Parham is recorded as farming an estate, which included Polebridge Farm, of 1,260 acres worked by 28 men, 13 boys. At the other end of the scale were single workers with their smallholdings. On a large farm, there were plough boys sometimes aged as young as 11, leading oxen pulling a plough, and women employed in seasonal fieldwork. It was also not unusual to see people working into their early 70s.

At the bottom of the before the First World War social scale there were people who declared themselves as paupers. It is difficult to challenge the accuracy of these figures because some almost destitute residents may have been unwilling to admit their circumstances or perhaps did not qualify for Parish Relief. Either way, the numbers indicate the level of deprivation between 1841 and 1911. Inexplicably, there appear to be no paupers in 1861.

The agricultural depression was largely due to the increase of food imports and the beginnings of agricultural mechanisation. It had a profound impact on rural communities and Sutton Veny was no exception. There was a significant increase in paupers – a total of 38 former agricultural workers had no work. This was partly because Warminster was unable to take significant advantage of the Industrial Revolution since the flow of the River Wylye was neither powerful enough to drive large scale manufacturing processes, nor wide enough to import the quantities of coal needed to power steam engines. Getting a job in the village was difficult at the best of times and, as Gertrude McCracken mentions in her memoirs,[26] the choice of employment was largely confined to working on the land or going into service. There were other openings but that was limited to a few articled clerkships, family businesses and apprenticeships. Self-employment was largely limited to retail, service, weaving and haulage.

Workers began to migrate to large towns. In 1750 only about 15% of the country's population lived in towns but by 1900 it was 85%. In Sutton Veny the population dropped from 881 in 1871 to 467 in 1981.[23]

Just before the outbreak of the First World War the village had three shops, two inns, an off-licence, post office, and eight supply services. However, with the arrival of hundreds of civilians building and servicing the army camp infrastructure and the thousands of troops in training, a wide range of additional commercial opportunities emerged. In time, three hutted cinemas were built and numerous makeshift timber and corrugated iron lock-up shops sprang up. The trade in bicycle hire was particularly buoyant.

The prosperity was, however, short lived, and with the departure of troops and the temporary businesses closing, village servicemen returning from the Front once more found it difficult to find work. For a while there was the dismantling of the local camps, hospital and railway line, but little else. Each Sunday evening some villagers cycled the 20 miles or so over to Netheravon to do similar work, but that did not last. The drift away from Sutton Veny continued.

There was no census in 1941, but after the war the population of the village continued to fall as it had after the First World War. The concept of commuting to work had become the norm with many travelling to Warminster by bicycle or bus, or by train to Bath and Salisbury. The Army garrison and workshops provided significant employment.

With the gradual increase in prosperity during the late 1950s and 60s, and with the growing affordability of motor cars, the populations in the villages began to increase, but not in Sutton Veny because, until the early 1970s, few new houses were built.

Modern businesses

T HE FORMER SECOND WORLD WAR army camp, the Deverill Road Trading Estate, is on the edge of the village and whilst not *in* the parish, companies operating there have the potential to impact significantly on the community. There are no issues with this at the moment but the arrival of certain industrial processes, generating significant traffic movement, noise and air pollution, could have a significant environmental effect unless they are effectively controlled; Sutton Veny is, after all, in a Conservation Area.

By the late 1950s, the War Office had no further use for the camp and it was sold. The buildings were stripped of anything of value and some left as roofless shells. The site was bought by Frank and Geoffrey Sykes, pioneer poultry breeders. Later West Wiltshire District Council took an interest in its potential for industrial starter units. The County Council objected because it did not comply with their Structure Plan but permission was given on appeal, subject to the condition that 32 acres of the site reverted to agricultural use.

In 1985 the company Sawa Ltd bought the site and set about tidying it up and marketing the remaining buildings as low cost, low rent industrial units. Some new units have been built and the demand for the original ones remains high. There are now 48 business, creating employment for over 130 people; all but one of the businesses are local.

Elsewhere in the village and at the end of the 1980s, West Wiltshire District Council wanted to encourage more new small businesses to become established, providing local employment. Sutton Veny was one such location and 12 compact units were built on the Norton Road Pound Barton Industrial Estate. Today they are all let with seven occupied by one company. Only one business is village based.

7
HOUSING

Development in the village

AFTER THE FIRST WORLD WAR the very gradual process of improving the quality of housing in the village began. Fifty-four former cottages were knocked down or merged to make 26 houses. Virtually no new homes were built.

The group of houses on the Norton Road named Sandfield was built by Warminster and Westbury Rural District Council in 1954. The original intention had been to have six houses, leaving room for a potential village hall at the rear. In the event, the cost of widening Bests Lane was too great and the hall proposal was abandoned; four additional houses were built instead. In the 1960s, 24 houses were built at Springhead at the east end of the village.

Greenhill House (original) and yard

In the 1980s some of the former farm buildings on both sides of Greenhill House, Norton Road (originally Greenhill Farmhouse), were cleared away or converted by private developers, making two small estates. Later, a barn was converted into a terrace of dwellings and named Campbell Place.

Over the road the former Greenhill House kitchen garden had been, for a while, a commercial market garden, but in time it was built over and developed as council bungalows for the elderly. It was thoughtfully named Everett Close, with a reference back to the Everett family. In the early 1980s five more private houses were built adjacent to this at Greenhill Gardens.

There was a further development in the 1980s at Walnut Close, and some infill on the High Street, but little else because the council's housing policy limited significant development in the village.

In 1981 there was an attempt to create a 'dream village' of 98 homes for the elderly in the grounds of Sutton Veny House but it was refused, again because it was against council policy.

Despite tight control of new housing schemes, the council continued to search for somewhere to build a small social housing development. By 1988 a number of sites were identified in the village but for one reason or another they were all unsuitable. Eventually, however, a site at the eastern end of Five Ash Lane was found. Six houses were built by the Sutton Hastoe Housing Association for local people connected with Sutton Veny or adjoining parishes. There were over 20 applicants. At the suggestion of the landowner, the development was named Imby Close, 'In My Back Yard'; a parody for 'Nimby'.

At the time of the 1998 Sutton Veny Village Appraisal (referred to elsewhere in this book), there was an undercurrent of resistance to new housing: 60% did not think there was a need for more housing. Paradoxically, about 40 people said that they wanted to remain and move within the village but were unable to find a house that they could afford to buy.

Parish Housing Needs Survey 2014

IN OCTOBER 2014 Wiltshire Council carried out a survey to investigate the affordable housing needs of the parish.[24] Almost 340 questionnaires were distributed and whilst about a third of the households replied, two thirds did not; suggesting that either they had no strong views one way or another or perhaps that they did not care.

Of the third who did respond, just under a quarter supported the principle of some new housing, with the most popular choice being a small development of cheap starter homes.

Whilst the survey was specifically carried out to assess *housing* needs, a number of interesting statistics emerged.

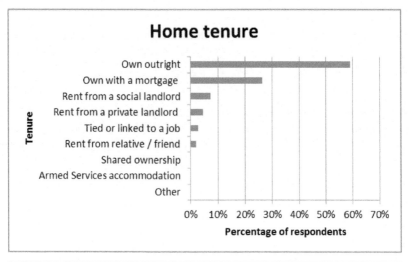

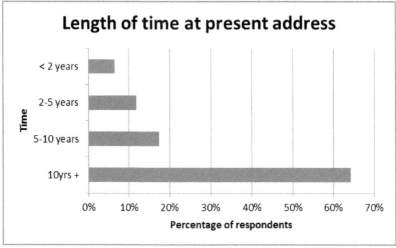

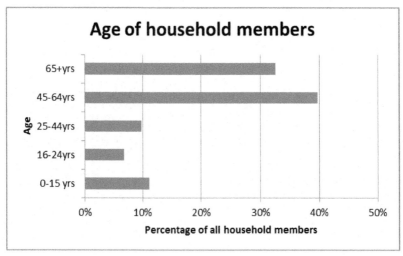

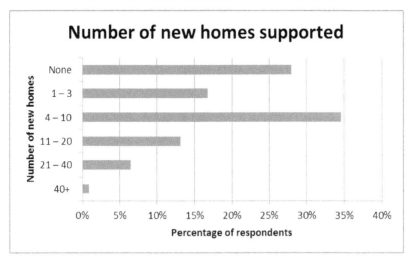

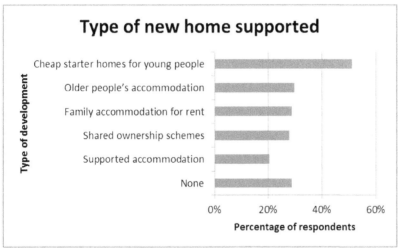

Persons in household	Distance to work				
	Up to 2 miles	2-10 miles	10-50 miles	50 miles +	Total
1	19	19	12	10	60
2	10	6	15	4	35
3	1	0	2	0	3
4	0	0	0	0	0
5	0	0	0	0	0
Total	30	25	14	14	98

8

COMMUNITY

THE POOR

L EGISLATION RELATING TO the support of the poor stems from the Tudor age and by the 19th century was firmly the responsibility of the Vestry (outlined in Chapter 2). It appointed the Overseer of the Poor to distribute money, food and clothing. The Parish Overseers' Account Books[25] show page after page of assistance handed out. For example:

19 Jun 1804. Mary Eacott to pay for learning to spin silk (she has promised not to be troublesome in the future).

19 Jul 1804. Paid for Iron letters Great and Small for marking Cattle etc. belonging to this Parish in case of invasion.

21 Jul 1804. Paying the man for getting Robert Screens out of the well. (Actually he was dead because there are several entries paying for the inquest, his coffin, funeral, burial and *beer for the men who carried the Corpse to the church.*

11 Apr 1814. Widow Elliott for a petticoat and Alice Price for a shift.

10 Aug 1818. Paid for taking Betty Hinton to Madhouse.

20 March 1830. Paid Mrs Roles for two cottages occupied by Paupers.

31 May 1833. Steven Everett… £17 taken up to send Immigrants to America.

The original Warminster Workhouse opened in 1727 to house the poor of Warminster and the surrounding 22 parishes including Sutton Veny. The original building, now The Snooty Fox public house in Fore Street Warminster, was replaced in 1837 with a purpose built workhouse at Sambourne. This closed in 1929 and the building has now been converted into a terrace of modern houses, The Beeches.

The aim of the workhouse was to discourage people from claiming Poor Relief and to achieve that, conditions were made harsh. The prospect of being sent there was one of utter dismay but for some, their poverty was so extreme that there was simply no alternative. The shame of being 'in the workhouse' extended beyond death – in Sutton Veny's Burial Registers the institution was known by the euphemism 33 Sambourne. A number of villagers are recorded as living there, but there appears to have been no more than nine men at any one time. Interestingly, most were unmarried and had previously worked either on the land or as servants. One inmate, John Butt, entered the workhouse in 1871 at the age of 53 and was still there 10 years later.

Apart from entering the workhouse, paupers had the option of applying for parish relief. There is a report in the Wiltshire Independent 30 July 1874 about the death of Robert Whatley in Warminster workhouse. He was a small village farmer and following the death of his wife, *he became abandoned and soon ran through his property. He had a wooden leg and was incapacitated and became vagabond, spending all the money he could get in drink and would frequently be found under hedges.*

The village nurse

AT A PARISH COUNCIL meeting on 31 March 1896, there was an edifying exchange of views about the appointment of a resident nurse for the village and, more particularly, who was going to pay the cost. One councillor, Mr Ball (a shopkeeper at what is now Prospect House opposite St John's)… *expressed a view that people could themselves afford to pay for any nursing that was required. By-and-by they would have to chew the people's food, and throw it against the wall ready for them to come and take it off. He would be pleased to support the suggestion if there was a necessity for it and that there was every provision for people to provide against sickness. If they were neglectful, then it was plenty good enough to go to the Workhouse.* Another councillor, Mr Pond (a farmer), said *a trained nurse would only do the nursing. What was wanted was a woman who could help in the house work as well. They were pretty well off in Sutton Veny as they had a good doctor near and the village was not far from the hospital.*

The issue appears to have dragged on for years and even in the 1920s there is reference to… *our raising money to have our own Queen's nurse. Someone gave a cottage and everyone contributed what they could to furnish it and set it up.* It is unclear if a resident Sutton Veny nurse was ever appointed.

Before the National Health Service was set up, most families paid a few pence 'surgery money' for the services of a doctor and free medicines. Most of the families were looked after by Dr Hinton from Heytesbury, a peppery little man who used to cycle around the village to see his patients.[26]

> **Dr Hinton had two great loves, cricket and gardening. He created a new variety of white sweet pea which he named after his wife. The National Sweet Pea Society archives record that Constance Hinton was the most popular variety of the 1920s. Specimens no longer exist.**

CRIME

> ### A Caution to Drivers of Waggons and Carts.
> I JOHN NEWMAN, of Sutton Veny, in the county of Wilts, labourer, having grofsly affronted CHARLES PENRUDDOCKE, of Compton Chamberlayne, in the faid county of Wilts, Efquire, by riding on my cart, and driving the fame on the public highway fo near his carriage, as greatly to endanger its being overturned, and afterwards by ufing infolent language, do, in this public manner, humbly beg his pardon for my offence, and acknowledge his lenity in forgiving me, on my paying the expence of this advertifement, and promife never to offend in like manner again.
> 347]   JOHN NEWMAN.

CRIME IN SUTTON VENY in the 18th and early 19th century, whilst not serious, was common. Most reflected the conditions of the poor with drunkenness, petty theft (flour, potatoes etc.) and poaching. Usually, a fine was imposed with sums which the average person would be unable to pay. William Jeffries was fined £5 for attempting to kill fish and a further £5 for possessing a pheasant. Samuel Prince was fined £20 for poaching. Since a labourer's weekly wage was typically 40p it is assumed that a custodial sentence would have been imposed leaving families to rely on Parish Relief.

Executions took place on Sutton Veny Common at the crest of the hill between Sutton Veny House and North Lodge on the Warminster Road. One, on 5 August 1783, was of Matthew Gardener and John Wheeler.[27] They had previously been found guilty of various crimes in and around Warminster but it was an attack on Benjamin Rebbeck of Stockton that proved to be the final straw; they were sentenced to death. *On the night before his death one of them made a confession before the Turnkey (gaoler) at Fisherton Jail in Salisbury. I saw a horse standing at the Pack Horse, with a sack on it full of something, which I took off and carried away. When I opened it I found it to be full of meat.*

With the government's desire to build and populate the colonies, many men and women received the sentence of transportation. Among the very first people in England to be transported to Australia were James Carpenter and John Grist, who were found guilty of stealing half a bag of wheat flour from John Gosney, Miller of Sutton Veny in 1788, they were sentenced to *be transported beyond the seas for a period of seven years.* They were held on a prison hulk for two years before being transported on 5 January 1791 with a group of 106 convicts in a flotilla of 11 vessels. They arrived in New South Wales six months later. It is not known if either returned as free men. In the following 50 years a further six Sutton Veny men suffered the same fate.

A constable is recorded as living in the village in 1841 and a police presence continued in a house rented from the Greenhill Estate until 1933 when the Police House was built in the High Street. The last resident village police constable was withdrawn in the 1960s although the police house was occupied by a police traffic patrol driver.

PASTIMES

The Alexander Field

The six acre field at the centre of the village is a facility which has played an important part in the community's outdoor social activities for almost 90 years. It was originally called Butcher's Field and the owner, Farmer HW Jeans, had allowed villagers to use it for recreation. After his death, Col the Hon Walter Alexander who lived at Polebridge, bought the field in 1928 to ensure its village use continued. He gave it to Salisbury Diocese, '…*for the purpose of playing cricket, football and other games…*' and '*for any other end or purpose which may promote the spiritual, intellectual, moral, social or physical welfare of the Members of the Church of England in the Parish or Diocese, but not necessarily to the exclusion of others…*'.

Whilst Salisbury Diocese is the controlling trustee, it is managed locally by administrative trustees, the rector and churchwardens of the ecclesiastical Parish of Sutton Veny. Formal leases and licences are in place for several regular village organisations and the trustees can make arrangements with individuals for temporary occasions such as weddings. Whilst only the controlling trustees can sell or lease any part of the field, it can only be with the agreement of the charity commissioners.

The Deed of Gift made allowance for half an acre *to be consecrated as a Churchyard burial place*, and that gift was partly redeemed in 2001 when the Bishop of Ramsbury consecrated a quarter of an acre as a churchyard extension.

The Village Hall

Although available for communal purposes, the Chapel Schoolroom, the Booker Hall Reading Room and the Primary School all lacked modern facilities – a proper hall was needed. An attempt to acquire a surplus First World War hut from the Army had come to nothing.

The project had initially begun in 1925 with a deposit of £65 into a bank account, and small sums and the profit from the 1952 Coronation celebrations had been added but there was little tangible progress.

In 1969 rector Roland Desch convened a public meeting to explore the possibility of having a purpose built village hall. A committee was set up to find ways of taking the project forward and fund raising began in earnest. A group of mothers started a children's club and a sponsored walk by the children raised £103 which instantly reinvigorated enthusiasm. The club entered floats in local carnivals, donating their prize money. In 1970, and for the following eight winters, the children rehearsed and acted in pantomimes which they performed in the February half-term holiday, adding the proceeds to the fund. Village Guy Fawkes night firework displays had begun and the committee raised money by selling hot dogs.

Salisbury Diocese agreed to sell a small part of the Alexander Field for a hall and fundraising efforts were stepped up.

It was decided to take advantage of the steady stream of summer holiday traffic heading down the A303 to the West Country. This venture involved over 50 people. A second-hand caravan was converted into a mobile kitchen with a big serving hatch; an old Calor gas stove was installed, utensils donated, supplies ordered and a trading licence granted. A 48 hour rota was drawn up ready for a trial run at the 1970 Easter weekend. One of the committee members was George Russell, a police officer who lived in the village. He encouraged patrol cars to stop in the layby not only for free cups of tea but to radio for replenishment supplies from the village. The venture was such a success that it was repeated on that Whitsun and summer bank holidays and the following year.

The estimated cost of the building was over £14,000. The Department of

> There is a delightful story of how Brig. John Platt was taking his turn on the caravan rota and approached a couple who had pulled over for a rest. He knocked on the car window, and they wound it down. He stuck his head in and bellowed across the noise of the traffic, at the top of his parade ground voice: *would you care for a cup of tea?* They jumped out of their skin with surprise. Whether they recovered enough to buy some tea was not reported.

Education and Science and Wiltshire County Council agreed to pay 75% of the cost. The contribution from the council had been made on condition that the hall could be let to the school during term time at a commercial rate. A subsequent government cut forced them to reduce their offer by £1,500 which was devastating but the project was saved by an interest-free loan from an anonymous villager. The building opened in October 1972.

Reading Room

THE PROVISION OF reading rooms were a national initiative founded with the aim of offering *places where the working men of a village may meet together for an evening's chat, without also being tempted into an evening's dissipation, ruinous alike in its*

Reading Room

effect upon body as well as soul. They were intended as an alternative to the public house and a place for the development of education.

In Sutton Veny the Reading Room appears to have been open each winter in a cottage rented for the season. However, in 1886 rector Arthur Booker converted an old wool store he owned into a permanent reading room and place for other parochial work (the door with a porch on the extreme right of this picture). It became known as the Booker Hall.

After he died in 1896, his trustees sold the building to the Church of England at the nominal sum of £100; the money having been given by his parishioners, friends and family *'who desired that the Reading Room might be a Memorial of his work at Sutton Veny and a help to the cause for which he laboured so earnestly during his whole life as parish priest'*.[28]

From records it is clear that the use of the building *struck an appropriate balance between providing a place sufficiently attractive to the labouring classes at the same time to ensure it was also a place for educational and moral advantage advancement'*. As the chairman of the Norton Bavant Reading Room put it, *'this is not a room for idle resort but for instruction, amusement and to pass a leisurely hour.* In view of his tone of sobriety, its position mid-way between The Woolpack and The Bell Inn will not have gone unnoticed.

The Booker Hall was sold after the village hall had been completed further down the high street and has now been incorporated in to the fabric of the adjoining house, the Furrows.

> One very dark winter evening. Gertrude McCracken's dad decided to walk to the pub in the next village, Corton. He had to go through an avenue of beech trees which had the reputation of being haunted. He heard footsteps behind him which seemed to stop and start, accompanied by a weird, indefinable sound. Dad began to feel nervous, so he lifted his walking stick, a hefty blackthorn, saying 'Joker or ghost, take this'. He crashed the stick against something solid. There was a shuffling, slithering noise, with an appalling unearthly moan. Poor Dad just stood there, shaking. Finally, he managed to control his hands and struck a match, and there at his feet lay a cow..

The Women's Institute

THE INAUGURAL MEETING of the Sutton Veny WI was held on 20 March 1920 in the chapel schoolroom. The first meeting following just over three weeks later, with a demonstration of making the Longleat Shoe (the local name given to an indoor house shoe). Whilst over the years the aims and objectives have shifted to reflect a changing society, the core activities remain largely unchanged, and it still provides its members with opportunities for learning, recreation and friendship.

The lectures and demonstrations on a wide range of subjects have continued over the years. The Sutton Veny Book, compiled by the Sutton Veny WI gives accounts of some of their activities on aspects of caring for the family. A subject one evening many years ago that today raises a smile was *The best way to amuse a man on a winter's evening.*

In the 1970s it had become necessary to adjust the road junction between Five Ash Lane and the Warminster Road. This created a small area locally referred to as The Green and in 2000 the WI celebrated its 80th anniversary by creating a much needed footpath between them both.

The Flower Show

DURING THE WINTER of 1966 a villager David Bunyan, had the idea for Sutton Veny to hold a flower show. A committee was formed and in July 1967 the first Sutton Veny and Norton Bavant Flower Show was held on the Alexander Field with only residents of the two villages being allowed to enter.

In later years other villages joined and the show became The Sutton Veny, Norton Bavant, Tytherington and Bishopstrow Flower Show. Both Heytesbury and Longbridge Deverill had their own annual shows.

Brig. John Platt approached the Royal Engineers in Warminster, for the loan of a tent. A large one, with trestle tables, was supplied free of charge and erected by soldiers as a training exercise. Although the hire of the tent itself cost nothing, money was still needed for schedules, entry forms and prize cards. In order to raise enough money to cover these and other costs, fundraising events were held throughout the preceding winter. Exhibitors' entry fees covered the prize monies. It was anticipated that the tent would not be big enough so the school lent a classroom for the flower displays.

There were over 300 entries and this encouraged the committee to plan another show the following year. That was also successful and in 1969 the committee held a Christmas Show in the school (the village hall had not yet been built). Only preserves, handicrafts, Christmas fare and children's exhibits were displayed but it was only moderately successful and after four years it was abandoned.

The Summer Show went from strength to strength with village residents taking their turn on the committee. In 1977 a large white marquee was hired to replace the dark green army tent.

In the late 1980s, after a few wet years, the show fell very short of money so local landowners were approached to make donations. Eton College, Boots Pension Fund and Lord Bath all sent donations, and money was also raised by the committee themselves by holding Saturday night discos. These proved very popular indeed with people coming from Warminster and beyond to enjoy the evening. The introduction of the May plant sale also proved a good source of income.

The cost of hiring the marquee later became so high that it was decided to make more use of it by holding at first a disco and later a barn dance on Show evening, with a 'Songs of Praise' service the following Sunday morning.

Bonfire night

THE ISSUE OF INJURIES caused by fireworks at private events had been a growing national concern for quite some years and increasingly, communities were encouraged to hold organised firework displays. In 1968 a bonfire and firework display was held on the Alexander Field with the costs being met by a local collection and the sale of hot food and drink. This annual event now run by the Village Hall continues to grow in popularity.

Cricket

THE 1887 GREENHILL ESTATE sale catalogue described 'the cricket ground' in a 15 acre field by the North Lodge but is not clear whether the village club actually played there. Sutton Veny Cricket Club certainly had fixtures in 1879 and again in 1904, because they played in the Warminster and District League. The list of club members then included a selection of names familiar from elsewhere in this book: Barter, Crouch, Cundick, Everett, Hinton and Varnon.

In 1907 the local newspaper reported that a young Oliver Lines (the village baker's son and later church organist), achieved a remarkable feat. He was bowling for the Sutton Veny second eleven against Emwell School (now the Minster) in Warminster; he got a Hat Trick (three wickets with three consecutive balls) twice in the same match.

Incidentally, Oliver is said to have made another record in the 1950s when, during a match, he hit a ball clean over St John's Church roof.

During a match at the Rectory park one Saturday afternoon in 1913, a fire broke

Bath Chronicle and Weekly Gazette. 26 July 1913

out in a terrace of four houses on the opposite side of the road. The teams were able to help neighbours bring out the household goods before the thatch caught fire but despite damming the Springhead stream to provide sufficient water to pump, the fire brigade was unable to save the building. The Park View houses now stand on the site.

The team's pavilion was a small green and white painted hut. Butcher's Field was just the other side of the hedge, so when Col. Alexander bought it for villagers in 1928 the team bodily lifted the pavilion over on to the new ground.

The club stopped playing in the 1960s but it was revived in 1974. It flourished, attracting players from beyond the village. The pavilion was extended and eventually rebuilt.

In 2000, the Australian High Commissioner was attending the ANZAC service and noticed the cricket ground over the churchyard wall with Andy Frost working on the wicket. They had a chat and the

The Australia-Sutton Veny cricket trophy

commissioner arranged to bring a team to play against the village. The Australia vs Sutton Veny match has become an annual fixture with the annual cricket match trophy at stake. Currently, honours are roughly even.

In 2008 the club merged with Heytesbury to form the Heytesbury and Sutton Veny Cricket Club.

Sutton Veny Cricket Team 1921

Fox hunting

> Fred Judd (b.1911) recounted that as a lad he would join the hunt staff playing quoits in the paddock by the kennels. An iron spike was driven into the ground and the quoits of cast steel weighing seven pounds (three kg) each would be thrown in an attempt to land it over the spike.

Fox hunting in the area has taken place since the beginning of the 17th century. The activity involves tracking, chasing and sometimes killing a fox by trained foxhounds with a group of followers usually on horseback, led by a Master of Hounds. The Hunt area referred to as a 'country', can extend over many square miles. Today the country is allocated and controlled by the Masters of Fox Hounds Association. The hunting season is from November until May.

Over the years, the land around the Sutton Veny parish has been under the control of several 'hunt countries'. In 1824 William Codrington brought his own hounds to Greenhill when he took over the South Wilts Hunt. Some 14 years later, the hunt was disbanded after he sold them to the Blackmore Vale Hunt.

John Everett inherited the Greenhill estate from his father and accepted an invitation to become Master of the West Wilts Hunt. In 1869 there were, once again, hounds in the village.

John Frederic Everett

A year or so later this merged with the South Wilts Hunt and with hounds kept at the Sutton Veny kennels, they hunted over their combined countries. Fourteen years later, John resigned his mastership writing in his resignation letter *owing to unexpected pecuniary loss*. He went on to say, however, that he had *generally found the guaranteed subscription sufficient to meet the expenses*.

Afterwards, hunting from Sutton Veny continued with a number of different masters.

During the Second World War, Charles and Daisy Fowle came to live at Greenhill Farmhouse. Charles was instrumental in the hunt's survival during an extremely difficult period, by providing stabling and horses for themselves and the hunt staff.

There are lots of country tales about the wily fox outwitting a hunt. Some think that they are made-up or have some explanation; this may be the case but not always. Peter McCracken recalls an incident his grandfather had told him. *I was digging a grave at St John's one day. You could tell the hunt was out by the sound of the hunting horn, hounds baying and the general commotion in the High Street; their blood was up. I took no notice cos you got used to it. Suddenly the fox appeared, ran past the grave I was diggin' and jumped into a tree right beside me. Soon after a huntsman called from the High Street asking if I had seen the fox. I told him I hadn't. He thanked me and rode on. The fox soon came down and trotted away, pausing to turn and look at me as if to say 'thanks'.*

It became more and more difficult to cover costs and, as a result, hunting out of Sutton Veny ceased in 1965 with Henry (Ben) Bennett-Shaw as the last Master of the Wylye Valley Hunt. The country was returned to the South and West Wilts, the Avon Vale and the Royal Artillery Hunts.

The kennel buildings have now gone but the name remains, given to the small block of houses on the site. The stables and the hunt servants' lodging rooms have been replaced by the Pound Barton Industrial Estate.

Hounds between the wars

The Bowls Club

T HE CLUB WAS established in 1904 and set up in the Rectory Park next to St John's Church. It was reached from the High Street by a path along the eastern wall of the churchyard. A fence and shallow ditch was made around the green with members using their own tools to clear the ground until sufficient funds were available for the club to buy its own. Mrs Geoffrey Lubbock of Greenhill gave several tons of topsoil to enable members to level and improve the playing surface.

Whist drives, lotteries and other fundraising helped raise enough money for a small wooden clubhouse to be built to accommodate about 30 members. Although some crockery had been donated, there was no electricity so water had to be heated by Calor gas. There were no toilets but an Elsan was provided for the ladies and a few sheets of corrugated iron at the back of the clubhouse for the gentlemen.

The playing surface had three bowling green rinks (parallel playing strips). Initially there were friendly matches against other local clubs and later the club entered the Wiltshire Three Rink League. It was active from the outset with strong and active support from Rectors Arthur Sewell and Eustace Chorley and, after the Rectory was sold in 1911 and the building became The Manor again, the new occupants Sir William Nicholson and Henry Goodall continued their support, both donating handsome silver competition cups.

By 1975 it was becoming difficult to get people to mow the green and as interest in the club dwindled, it was wound up in March 1979, with the assets being sold off and the land reverting to pasture.

Gay Donald was a race horse owned by Philip Burt (Glebe Farm). Trained by Jim Ford, he was entered in the Cheltenham Gold Cup in 1955 as long-shot. Ridden by Tony Grantham (who usually rode for the Queen Mother). The horse won at 33-1, beating the previous Gold Winner Four Ten, into second place by 10 lengths.
Gay Donald was it seems, a very friendly and idiosyncratic horse who loved Liquorice Allsorts and tucking into his trainer's sardine sandwiches for lunch on away days..

The Village Appraisal 1998

I N 1998 VILLAGERS took part in an appraisal prompted by a government initiative, the Rural Action for the Environment. Its purpose was to identify villagers' likes and dislikes about the village and what facilities they would like to see provided. It was designed to inform the local and other authorities when considering projects impacting on Sutton Veny. The appraisal covered a wide range of elements such as housing, industry, highways and transport but also some specific village facilities such as the Parish Council, the church, village hall and the Alexander Memorial Field. In all it gave a rounded picture of what villagers thought of their community and felt about its future. 75% responded.

Looking at the findings 30 years after the appraisal, it is interesting to note how attitudes have changed. For instance:

Over 50% of villagers supported the introduction of mains gas to the village. Almost 60% supported mains drainage, over 20% would definitely not support.

The idea of a public telephone box at the Springhead end of the village had strong support. 60% of respondents thought it was needed, while 28% considered it unnecessary. 78% wanted a village post office.

Villagers were not fans of an information superhighway with 70% suggesting internet speed should be improved; a definite thumbs down.

More than 50% of people thought they would buy staple products or services from a shop if it could be re-established. These villagers would buy fresh bread, groceries, milk and dairy produce, newspapers and use the post office with its GIRO services frequently or very frequently.

The report finishes with a quote from one of the respondents: *I think that we are extremely lucky to live in this village. Modern life and work mean that inevitably people have less time to devote to community matters and we must work hard to preserve what we have, with many of us, I fear, taking too much for granted. Regretting its passing is a thing I can see happening unless we are careful and make an effort.*

9
WAR

FIRST WORLD WAR

SOON AFTER THE outbreak of war, the first of 10,000 troops started to arrive in the village.[29] Initially they were accommodated under canvas and in 1915, hutted camps were erected each side of the Bishopstrow Road. The camp had a branch railway line from Heytesbury through to Longbridge Deverill to carry building materials and, later, the soldiers.

> I think that the Scots made a great impression in my childish mind. I remember so vividly when in full dress, they marched through the village. It was a warm, sunny day and it seemed as if their spats and kilts moved as one. They moved with their pipes and I stood there speechless, as the sound of the pipes gradually moved away. I gave a great sigh and said, 'Coo, if I grow ever so old, quite fifty, I shall always remember this day'. [26]

Swirling kilts as long as I live

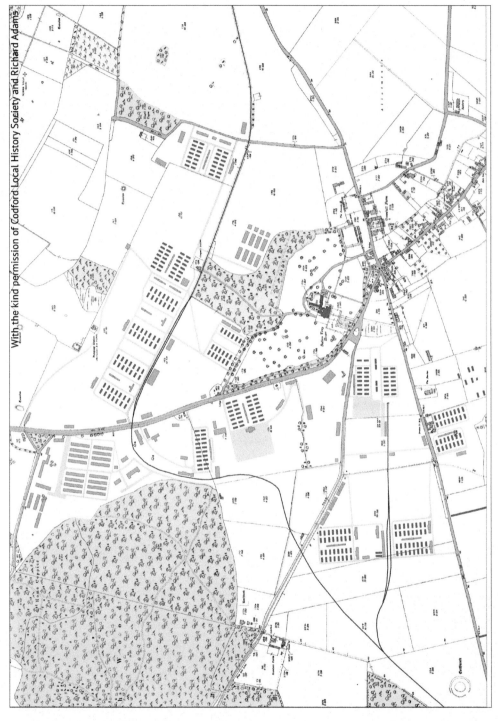

With the kind permission of Codford Local History Society and Richard Adams

Sutton Veny camp 1916

The huts were basic – merely brick piers, wooden planked walls lined with asbestos and heavy paper and a corrugated iron roof. They were built quickly with unskilled labour so the general workmanship was poor. They required continual maintenance and were cold and damp, but at least each hut had one stove.

Bath Chronicle and Weekly Gazette. 12 August 1916

Water was piped from a borehole at Greenhill and primitive sewage pits dug within each camp. Subsequently a rudimentary treatment facility was built at the rear of

Cow Down Butts

the village behind cottages on Deverill Road – an arrangement which later was to cause health problems.

The farmland around Sutton Veny was requisitioned for training. In addition to basic soldiering skills of marching and shooting, there was instruction in digging, living in trenches and learning the principles of basic mining and ground engineering. A rifle range was set up in the area west of The Beeches on Deverill Road, with targets against the base of the hill at Cow Down. The sniper range firing point was set up in the area just to the west of Walnut Close, giving an approximate range of 1,000 yards to the same targets.

Hospital main gate

The 1,200 bed Sutton Veny Military Hospital was north of the camp on the Bishopstrow Road and became functional by about September 1915. Initially the patients were British soldiers and German POWs. ANZAC troops began to arrive early 1917, first gradually and then in much greater numbers. When the war ended, Australian troops continued to be treated there and its name was changed to the First Australian General Hospital; this was the time when the Spanish flu epidemic took hold.

Small shops established themselves wherever they could, particularly on the northern edge of the village, selling all sorts of necessities and small luxuries to the soldiers. Greenhill House was a staff headquarters but subsequently became a YMCA. Both the Woolpack and the Bell did a healthy trade and there were regular minor disturbances between the soldiers and the local youths, especially at the end of the evening.

A Pals battalion was made up of men who had enlisted together in local recruitment drives, with the promise that rather than being arbitrarily allocated to battalions, they would be able to serve alongside their friends, neighbours and colleagues (pals). Among the troops passing through the camp was a Pals battalion from the Tyneside Irish Brigade from Newcastle-upon-Tyne in 1914. Mr P O'Rorke from the Tyneside Irish Committee visited Sutton Veny and wrote:

The first impression one gets, on approaching in the darkness the almost endless rows of huts that afford such excellent accommodation for the troops, is that of a northern mining village in the days when the wooden structures were practically the only dwellings of the northern miners; but here the resemblance ends. These temporary billets, scattered in well ordered regularity over the wide expanse of moorland, leave nothing in wanting in the shape of comfort for the soldiers. Lighted throughout by electricity and fitted up with everything necessary for military purposes they are, even to the eye of a mere civilian, a wonderful improvement on the canvass camp.

It rained nearly every day during the winter of 1915/1916 and there was thick, sticky mud everywhere. This reduced morale and made the simplest of outdoor tasks hard and difficult work.

One of the most famous cartoons of the war was drawn in Sutton Veny. *Well, if you knows of a better 'ole, go to it!* was drawn by Bruce Bairnsfather whilst attached to the 34th Division as a Machine Gun Officer stationed at Greenhill, in October 1915.

During the war there were three cinemas in the village. The first was halfway along Five Ash Lane, the second was in the High Street at the corner of Dymocks Lane and the third was by the small quarry at the junction of the Deverill Road and Warminster Road. The latter was burnt down one evening by soldiers (rumoured to be Tyneside Irish) about to go to France. The projector broke and the wife of the owner could not reimburse money because her husband had left with the takings. They were offered free tickets for the following evening but that was no use because many were leaving for France the following day. The troops set fire to the cinema, dragged the piano

"Well, if you knows of a better 'ole, go to it."

outside and sang songs. Then ending with 'Keep the Home Fires Burning', they threw the piano on the fire and left. As they did, barrels of engine oil under the stage exploded.

The event was recalled by Muriel, the daughter of CSM Erett, who was living in a thatched cottage near the camp. She remembered the arrival of the Sutton Veny fire brigade[30]: ... *an old man very out of breath, with a bucket, a short length of hose and a pump. By the time he got there the cinema had burnt to the ground.*

The British troops were eventually moved out and troops from the Australian Imperial Force (the Australian Expeditionary Force) occupied a number of camps in the Valley with, in December 1916, No. 1 Australian Command Depot being stationed in Sutton Veny. It remained until the end of the war.

Around the same time, soldiers from Canada and New Zealand moved in to Codford and the Wylye Valley. Not long after they arrived, a fight started between all three nationalities near Pine Cottages at the eastern edge of the village on the Sutton Parva Road. Two men were killed and it was rumoured 40 were injured. The New

Zealanders were moved onto Salisbury Plain and the Canadians transferred elsewhere.[31]

There were many tense exchanges between the Australians and the local inhabitants mainly from Warminster. One Australian wrote of his experiences well after the war:

The Australians evidently had a bad name then, because the day we arrived the shops in Warminster were shut and even the doormats were taken inside. The people tried to get Warminster out of bounds to the Australians but the boys wouldn't have that and took it upon themselves to march in, in a body, and the out of bounds notice was lifted...our little group was alright and the people were glad that we came as we had plenty of money to spend...

A number of civilians were caught trafficking Army equipment. A newsletter from 60th (London) Divisional Cyclist Company Old Comrades Association recounts:

An amusing incident occurred at Sutton Veny after the main body of the Company went to France. I was one of those left behind and we did roaming guard (in pairs) around the camp at night on the look out for civilian scroungers of W.D property.

One night the other bloke and I heard clinking of metal and shone our torches and picked up a man and a boy pinching old bicycle frames. On questioning the man, he replied to the effect – they didn't belong to anybody, do they? When we told him what was what, we also told him we would see him and his boy off the site and to the village. A voice nearby said 'You'd better do what the young soldier says'. Switching our lights around, we discovered the village constable. We thoroughly enjoyed marching the trio down the road to Sutton Veny, particularly the village bobby who was as much involved as the other two.

Between 1916 and 1917 many British battalions occupied camps to hone their skills prior to leaving for France. Inevitably there were training accidents; one in particular was a fatality in 1916 when George Pearce 2/18th London Regiment (the London Irish), was operating a West Spring gun (a bomb-throwing catapult). Pearce thought he had not activated the fuse and as he leant over the gun it went off.

Civilian internment and military prison camps were established in Wiltshire attached to military bases and airfields. They were guarded by the Royal Defence Corps, consisting of personnel too old or medically unfit for active front line service. In 1917 a Home Office report identified local camps at Bulford, Chiseldon, Codford, Larkhill, Fovant, Perham Down, Yatesbury and Sutton Veny. Local labour was in short supply and as the war continued, prisoners were used. There were 200 German prisoners in Sutton Veny who worked in the local fields and as hospital orderlies, but in time their own camp had become uninhabitable through lack of maintenance and they had to move out. German patients continued to be accommodated in guarded wards.

The Westbury Journal, 21 July 1916, reported:

A number of wounded German prisoners were expected to arrive at Warminster at about 2 o'clock on Friday afternoon and a large crowd assembled along Station Road and East Street in expectation. As it happened, however, those who had sufficient patience, were destined to wait till after 5 o'clock before the men arrived. Unshaven and with their clothing

> During the war, rumours were rife about spies and spying. George Hacker was a school attendance officer who lived at Sutton End. He would come over to the school as part of his official duties but suspicions were aroused when he increased these from once to twice a month whilst at the same time a special interest in the military camps. In 1916, the rumour was that he had been arrested and subsequently shot at the Tower of London. There is no record of his name among the 11 spies who were executed there – he was probably the victim of local gossip and suspicion. In fact, he died in Surrey in 1945.[26]

covered with mud, they presented a very repulsive appearance.

A fortnight later, on 12th August 1916, the Bath Chronicle and Weekly Gazette has a contrasting description:

About 70 German convalescent prisoners of war were conveyed from Sutton Veny Military Hospital to an internment camp in another part of the country. They arrived at Warminster looking war-worn and war-stained, and ill-fed, but they departed from Warminster G.W.R. station, looking far more healthy and apparently in good spirits. They marched briskly between the guard, who carried fixed bayonets, and on the arrival of the 1.35 p.m. train they were accommodated in two specially reserved corridor coaches in the front part of the train.

Many soldiers convalesced in Sutton Veny Military Hospital after being wounded in France. There were a number of suicides, an example from the Western Daily Press on 15 September 1917:

A verdict of 'Suicide while of unsound mind' was returned at an inquest on the body of Pte William Charles Trevarthen, of the Wilts Regiment. He was found in a wood near the camp with a gash in the throat, evidently self-inflicted with a razor.

There is no record of him being buried in the war graves so presumably, as with some other British patients who did not survive, his remains were returned home.

There was a crime in Sutton Veny in 1917 which was notable as being one of the first crimes to secure a conviction using ballistic tests:

Corporal Joseph Durkin, an Australian, shared a hut with another soldier, Verney Asser. Both of them were attracted to a local girl. In November 1917, two shots were heard and Durkin's body was discovered with a bullet wound to the cheek. The police reconstructed the scene (which involved firing shots into legs and shoulders of mutton to gauge the trajectory of the bullets and note the resulting damage). They concluded that he had been murdered. Suspicion fell on Asser, who claimed that had been woken up by the shot. But his bed appeared not to have been slept in and he was fully dressed. Verney Asser was tried at Devizes Assizes, convicted and hanged at Shepton Mallet prison.

At the end of the war thousands of Australians remained in the area to prepare for civilian life while awaiting discharge and passage home. In January 1919, No. 1 Australian General Hospital relocated at the camp.

As they left, the huts were gradually demolished, the railway taken up and the village slowly began to return to peacetime farming.

This apple tree is all that remains of an orchard that was being planted up on the day, in 1918, when a boy raced around the village on his bike shouting the news that the war had ended.

THE SECOND WORLD WAR

David Hobbs describes part of a letter he came across written about his father Peter by his uncle Paul, both of whom who were fighting in North Africa in 1942: After Rommel's forces had moved on following the Battle of Gazala in May, Paul heard that Peter had been wounded and taken to a hospital in Tobruk. Having searched them all and not found his brother, he made further enquiries and was told where he had last been seen. He went off into the desert and found the armoured car containing the bodies of Peter and his driver. With the help of a couple of South African soldiers, they buried them both where they had fallen. Paul was later killed in Tunisia 1943.

The Second World War had a different effect on the parish than the First World War. As before, troops were stationed just outside Sutton Veny and they mixed with the population, but their visual, social and economic impact was different. There were no rows of wooden huts, there was no hospital, no railway and no trench digging; the servicemen were being trained for a different kind of conflict.

Surprisingly, little has come to light about the war's impact on the parish; there are no maps and plans available and virtually no regimental records. However, there are villagers today who remember actual events of this time and whilst some childhood recollections can become cloudy, most remain as vivid as ever. Some are woven into this chapter and several are repeated elsewhere almost verbatim.

Lodgers renting rooms came and went but they had little effect on local traders because there was simply nothing to be had in the shops.

It might have been expected that the former First World War camp sites were re-established, but they had more or less been completely removed; in any event, it would have been quicker to build new camps on new and previously undisturbed ground.

In late 1939, fields on both sides of the Deverill Road were requisitioned and the Pioneer Corps hastily built two brick camps, laid out randomly to limit the risk of damage from pattern bombing. The units that occupied these varied as military requirements fluctuated; initially the southern camp (the present trading estate) was used for light armoured vehicles training.

Royal Observer Corps post

A ROYAL OBSERVER CORPS observation post was set up at the southern end of Dymocks Lane. There are no photos of it but childhood memories suggest that it was a simple wooden platform 8 or 10 feet off the ground, with a safety rail around the edge giving a clear view, unobscured by hedges. It was manned by local volunteers equipped with a telephone, binoculars, a mounted rangefinder with a series of template silhouettes of aircraft, all stored in a nearby wooden hut.

After the war the platform and installation was abandoned and eventually dismantled. During the Cold War, in about 1959, an underground bunker was built on the site to monitor fall-out following a nuclear attack. In 1968 it was decommissioned and today, whilst limited above-ground features remain, it is now private property and remains sealed shut.

Elsewhere, hardened field defences were erected to hinder an advancing enemy. An anti-tank trap was dug south west from Bishopstrow, crossing Five Ash Lane and south past Raxters Farm alongside Southleigh Woods. It was about two miles long and 6 - 10 feet deep with earth piled up on the northern side; it would have made a formidable obstacle.

There were no pillboxes in the parish itself but four were built on the boundary: near the railway bridge on the road to Heytesbury (the A36 roundabout), on the approach to Norton Bavant village, near Raxters Farm and on the edge of Southleigh Woods.

Pillbox on the edge of Southleigh Woods

Home Guard

THE HOME GUARD was formed in early 1940. It consisted of men aged between 17 and 65 who, for some reason, were not serving in the regular forces.

There is no escaping that today they are typified by a TV comedy series and as a consequence, their function is largely misunderstood. It was to harass the enemy following an invasion; they were not intended to be a significant fighting force.

The Sutton Veny Home Guard platoon was commanded by Brig Gen (Retired) Reginald Hobbs of Little Newnham.

US Troops

With the United States joining the conflict in 1941/2, their forces began training on the Downs and Salisbury Plain. Again, records of which units were stationed in the village are limited but US Army archives contain some letters and diaries of some of the personnel who have cause to remember their time in *little age-old English villages with quaint names and odd, meandering streets of Camp Sutton Veny.*

143 Company Royal Engineers occupied a small camp in Bests Lane at the beginning of the war and later, additional Nissen huts were built by the US Army for segregated black servicemen.

Sutton Veny Home Guard platoon (officer unknown)

We're ready for 'em!

The US troops adjusted to life in the village, brightening the drab existence of a weary community. Their generosity towards the children was greatly appreciated; one villager remembers that occasionally, food and other goods were put into a cardboard box, but sometimes carbolic soap had been included, which permeated everything including the sweets. The black Americans gave one particularly memorable Christmas party in 1944 with wonderful food and ... *balloons*!

Best Lane Nissen Huts

To mark the wartime presence of US troops in the village, a plaque has been placed in a small garden in the High Street at Hill Road on a site near where the Pound was once located. A plaque erected in 1994, remembers the Third Armoured Division.

David Eyres recalls that as a choirboy, seeing the soldiers filling the church one Sunday morning to the extent that when the pews were full, chairs were brought in to completely fill the aisles... *you could have walked out of the church across the top of their heads.*

Site of Third Armoured Division plaque

Life in wartime Sutton Veny

I N SEPTEMBER 1940, 73-year-old Edward Lane from Sevenoaks in Kent came to Sutton Veny to work at the Army Pay Office at Deverill Road camp. The following extracts from some of his letters home give a glimpse of his experience:

This is a tiny village, one post office and one shop - not even a butcher. It's about half a mile from the camps. We start at 7.15am, have half an hour for lunch and are supposed to finish at 6 but it's usually 6.30 before one can get away.

I am not sure I can hold this job down. Tremendous lot of clerical work to be done, figures galore all in triplicate and all the time men coming for all sorts of things. Their wages all to be made out and paid weekly and the government wanting full particulars for employment forms etc.

It's all outside sanitation here. It's always smelly.

There are two pubs, not very nice ones, nor do I care much for the beer they stock. Inside sanitation is unknown – one of my tribulations is connected with this, another is to understand the dialect. They talk as if their mouths were full of food.

I am now fixed at Mrs Riley's (76 High Street), 25 shillings bed and breakfast. There is no bath and as far as I can find out baths are very scarce. I've got to get other digs . . .

On Saturday I went to Warminster for a much needed bath and hot lunch. I'm moving to other rooms, Mrs Hicks (77 High Street), she can give me a hot meal at night and some sort of a bath but I think on Saturdays I shall treat myself to a real one in Warminster.

Went to Salisbury on the bus. A pretty drive along the Wylye river which is being used to flood parts and has gun pits here and there. Salisbury was a teeming mob of troops mainly Aussies and natives of the surrounding parts. The women were either pushing prams or soon would be. You should have seen Woolworths, Timothy Whites and Marks and Spencer. All adjoin each other and were one struggling mass of people. I caught a bus back at 5pm and had to stand for more than half way.

This place is much more exposed than Sevenoaks. The winds just sweep in. Some troops are to move into this camp soon, not that everything is ready but I suppose it is better than under canvas in this weather. As there is only half an hour for lunch I never get a hot one except Saturday and Sunday. Fowls and rabbits are cheaper here than at Sevenoaks.

I am now living over a small general shop. It has a bath and cold water. Hot water has to be carried. To get there I have to go through someone else's room. My bedroom is quite a snug little room, I have the use of the sitting room. I am to pay 35 shillings a week, this includes full board, sanitation is outside but so it is all over the village. The wireless is in the kitchen and I am just off there to listen to the 9 o'clock [News].

Mike Coward remembers an incident on 25 September 1940:

Sitting in school one September watching the clock for time to go home for dinner, we were all suddenly scared by the terrific noise of aeroplanes going very low overhead toward Shaftesbury. It was a German aircraft, clearly in trouble and going to crash. It was being closely chased by an RAF fighter.

I got home and found my father and Bill Vincent ready at the front gate with the pony cart. We all got in and off we went up the hill and down to Hammersmith. When we arrived, there were already people on the hill above Well Bottom at the scene of the crash. The pilot had in fact made a successful forced landing. I have very clear memory of the curved propeller tips. The aircraft was a two crew Messerschmitt Bf.110, a twin engine fighter that was withdrawn from daylight operations fairly early in the war, being vulnerable during daylight, but went on to be a successful night fighter. The pilot was unhurt but the second man had been killed by gunfire. I tried to have a look in the shattered rear canopy but was ordered away.

Mike remembers his father Dennis (known as 'Farmer') telling him of another incident on 24 April 1944 involving a Junker JU88A that had crashed earlier that night near Hill Deverill. Whilst the aircraft didn't actually crash in Sutton Veny, there is nonetheless an association with it.

My father kept cows down at Baggs Farm. He was cycling down one early morning to milk them and on passing Glebe Farm, heard Tony Burt's dogs barking and he saw across the fields, a parachute strung up in the beech trees below the Hanging with barking dogs on the ground nearby. The old man in spite of being a Lance Corporal in the Home Guard, decided that milking his cows was a better idea than heroics under the beech trees.

It transpires that the airman's name was *Unteroffizier* (sergeant) Johann Agten. He was the aircraft observer and subsequently surrendered to Home Guardsman farmer Philip Burt who found him with a wounded leg.

A more full version of the aircraft story is at Appendix 2.

There was a further incident later that morning involving a different airman:

Cycling back home at about 8 am after milking, Dennis spoke to his neighbour Ida Bull at 1 Park View. She was much exercised because somebody had used her water butt (which was her source of domestic water) to wash themselves and there was evidence of blood around. Subsequently, an enemy parachutist was arrested near Milestone Cottage in Tytherington and it was thought that it was he who had cleaned himself up and then wandered down to Tytherington in spite of the area swarming with Army and Home Guard.

WAR CASUALTIES

War graves

IN JANUARY 1919, the First Australian General Hospital transferred from Rouen to Sutton Veny, replacing the existing Military Hospital.

Having survived the war, the 1918-1919 Spanish Influenza pandemic was a devastating blow for the troops waiting to return home. Of the patients who died in the hospital throughout the entire war period, 50% (85) *died of sickness* during the three months of October and November 1918 and February 1919 (there was a lull during December).

There are 169 war graves in St John's graveyard, 140 of which are Australian soldiers. Alongside them are several female nurses and a nurse from the Second World War. Their memory is honoured on two separate occasions in the village: by schoolchildren on ANZAC Day itself (25 April), which is described in chapter 5 and in a Service of Remembrance, held on the Sunday nearest 25 April. This is attended by villagers, representatives of organisations with links to the military, and the Australian and New Zealand High Commissions.

ANZAC Remembrance Service 2017

The ANZAC Cemetery 1919

The part played by the schoolchildren and their own memorial service each ANZAC Day, is mentioned in the Primary School chapter of this book.

In her memoirs[31], Gertrude McCracken (b.1907) recalled, *...there had been an occasional military funeral in the village; the bearing party marching with arms reversed and*

Commonwealth War Graves Commission cemetery 2017

the coffin draped with the Union Jack. So many soldiers died of the influenza that the coffins were sometimes stacked in the wood behind the hospital.

By this time, many of the villagers had received one of the dreaded 'We deeply regret' telegrams, and the number of funerals held each day increased the grief of the people in the village. It was decided to minimise this by having the band and bearing party remain at the church instead of marching through the street. The coffins were taken to the church two or three at a time.

Although at one level each headstone marks the grave of yet another serviceman, it is as well to remember that each was an individual, leaving behind bewildered family and friends. This is the story of but one.

The story of Private Arthur Parkes

THE COMMONWEALTH WAR CEMETERY has a constant trickle of visitors, with some occasionally leaving a token of respect or remembrance. As with all the graves, there is a story for each person buried there: their family, their circumstances, how they came to rest in our village and the grief with which the news of their death was received. Here is one story of a soldier who served with the 40th Battalion Australian Infantry.

It started simply enough but as sometimes happens, one piece of information led to the discovery of another ...

One summer's evening in 2015, a villager noticed a man sitting on a bench in the churchyard and asked if he could help. He was a student on an Australian university course studying elements of the First World War. During his studies, he had come across the story of an ANZAC soldier, Arthur Luttrell, who was recorded as being buried in Sutton Veny. It seems that the soldier's mother, Emily, had wanted to visit her son's grave but she could not afford the cost of passage from Australia. He had come to put a wreath on the grave on her behalf, but had been unable to find it and laid his wreath at the Cross of Sacrifice instead.

There the story should have ended but the following day, the visitor emailed saying that he had the wrong name – Arthur's correct surname was *Parkes*. Sure enough, Private A.L. Parkes is indeed in the cemetery.

The villager removed the wreath from the cross and put it on Arthur's grave. As he did, a message card fell out and, with the visitor's agreement, we can share what it said:

Arthur:

> *You died never knowing the grief of your mother nor of how she tried to visit your resting place. She wanted to pay her respects and to honour your sacrifice. But circumstances thwarted her attempts. Know that she never stopped trying to get over to see your grave. Know also that she never stopped*

loving you.

Emily:

You died with a heavy heart knowing that you never managed to travel to England and to honour your son. You never stopped trying to get here and grieved for him as a mother who cared for her son would. You never stopped loving him. You never stopped trying to get the authorities to grant you assisted passage to see your son's final resting place.

Emily and Arthur:

With this wreath, the circle is completed.

With this wreath Emily, you are finally honouring your beloved son Arthur.

With this wreath Arthur, you are honoured by your beloved mother Emily.

The love which held you together is complete.

Your souls may now rest in peace.

Arthur Parkes' grave

Some weeks later, when the wreath had faded, the villager buried the card at the foot of Arthur's headstone.

Arthur was awaiting repatriation (the Armistice had been two months earlier) and had been posted to No. 1 Command Depot at Sutton Veny on 1 January 1919. Instead of repatriation, however, he was admitted to the Australian General Hospital at

Sutton Veny, dangerously ill with Spanish flu. He died on 5 February 1919. He was one of seven to be buried a few days later.

Emily had repeatedly pleaded an assisted passage from the Australian government. In a letter she says: *Please pardon me for taking the liberty of writing. If you could see your way to help me, I would deem it one of the greatest favours of my life.* The letter finishes with, *Trusting I am not asking too much from you. There was seven of our sons went to the war. Surely I have won the right to ask such a small favour.*

Unlike some other countries the Australian Government refused every application to subsidise pilgrimages abroad. A memorandum was drafted for the Prime Minister: … *it would be rather dangerous to accede to such requests. The deaths overseas numbered 58,854 and burials took place in many different countries. There is a danger of such privileges being abused.* She never did visit her son's grave.[33]

Having been privileged to glimpse, as it were, into a very personal element of Arthur Parkes' family, more information has come to light about him, this time his service record:

Alfred (Arthur) Leslie Parkes was born in 1890 at Rixes Creek, New South Wales to parents Francis and Emily J. Parkes. When he enlisted, he declared that he was a blacksmith from Hobart, Tasmania, aged 26 years and married with two children.

He sailed from Melbourne in October 1916. During the voyage on the troopship, he was given 168 hours detention for stealing.

He disembarked at Devonport in December 1916 and with reinforcements being given only basic training in Australia, completed his at Durrington and on Salisbury Plain.

Arthur sailed to France on 3 May 1917 and the next day marched to the military camp at Etaples (about 50 miles down the coast from Calais). Precisely where he saw action is not known, but four weeks later he suffered a gunshot wound to his left knee. He recovered and re-joined his unit on 5 June only to be wounded lightly a second time after two weeks.

On 3 October 1917, he received a shrapnel wound to his back and was returned to England for treatment. On discharge from hospital and convalescence, he was sent to the Overseas Training Brigade at Longbridge Deverill in March 1918.

He returned to his Battalion at Rouelles, France on 5 April only to be wounded a fourth time two weeks later but was able to remain on duty.

Arthur was wounded a fifth time with a bullet wound to his hand on 7 August 1918 and was returned to England. Although the wound healed, he was left with the tendon of his ring finger severed. The disability was permanent and he was medically reclassified fit for Home Service only.

The War Memorial

A FTER THE FIRST WORLD WAR an overwhelming desire grew nationally to remember and commemorate those who had died. Across the country memorials began to be erected, not under government, civic or church patronage, but by public and private subscription. In a village, they were generally placed in a central position. In Sutton Veny the site at the front of St John's churchyard, overlooking the High Street, was chosen.

On 20 February 1920, the Warminster and Westbury Journal reported:

The prime idea of sacrifice in its many variations is proved to be the gain of some benefit by the surrender of something of value, and the surrender was their own lives. This is what 15 sons of Sutton Veny did during the Great War, and on Sunday afternoon a beautiful Memorial was dedicated and unveiled in the village churchyard to perpetuate the memory of these worthy and gallant men whose sacrifice was the supreme one.

The memorial takes the form of a large monument built on a base of four steps on which rest a square with four panels and a high circular column, which is finished off with a cross. The whole of the monument is composed of the best Portland stone, and it reflects much credit on Mr Strong, of Portway, Warminster, who designed and erected it. The memorial stands close to the road and the panel opposite the road is inscribed to 'The Glory of God and in honour of the men of this village who fell in the Great War 1914 – 1919' and on the other three panels are the names of the 15 men who died that their homeland may be liberated from the oppression of an envious foe.

The memorial cost £170 and of this, a portion was raised by house-to-house collections in the village.

There were no formal rules about which names could be inscribed on the memorial – it was a local decision prompted by advertisements in the papers, local knowledge and word of mouth. Whilst sons and daughters of the village were clearly eligible for inclusion, there were others that had been born elsewhere and happened to live in the village when they marched to war, there were yet others whose parents may have lived in the village for only a short while, and so on. For these reasons, it is not uncommon for individuals to have been overlooked and arguably, a further five or six additional names could, or should, have been added. It is not known how many from the parish enlisted nor how many of them failed to return. The war memorial honours 15 servicemen killed in the First World War and a further seven in the Second World War. They are all named at Appendix 3.

A STROLL AROUND THE VILLAGE

Sutton Veny House

Sutton Veny House

WILLIAM HINTON OF BISHOPSTROW, a clothier, was granted ownership of the land and buildings at Greenhill under the Enclosure Award 1804. He is believed to have either enlarged an existing building or built a replacement.

On his death in 1816, his only daughter, Ann Hinton inherited the estate and let the land to a farmer, James Brown. The terms of the tenancy agreement give an insight into land husbandry at the time: … all harvest to be stored there, dung to be used on that land only. The tenant to practise the three field system according to the best rules of good husbandry. Not to sow two successive crops of the same kind of corn grain, pulses or roots. To allow no killing of game or trespass...

Ann died in 1831, and her executors leased the estate to Isabella Fane. The whole of the Greenhill estate was bought by Joseph Everett in 1853, a partner in the Bank

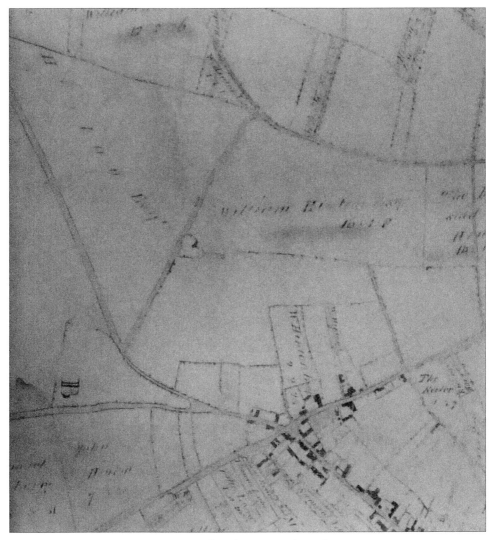

Greenhill Enclosure Award 1804

of Everett and Co. and a member of Heytesbury and Upton Lovell wool and cloth processing family.

Joseph enhanced the home park surrounding the house with specimen trees and woodland walks. He established a large walled kitchen garden with a lofty double 61 feet long vinery. Within a few years he had built two lodges, a number of staff cottages, Greenhill Farmhouse and a range of contemporary farm buildings, stables and kennels for the hunt.

Joseph's son, John Frederic, inherited the estate when his father died in 1865. John was a magistrate, a Lt. Col. of Volunteers and Master of Foxhounds. He was declared bankrupt in 1883.

Frances Everett

Joseph Everett

In 1887 an attempt to sell the estate was unsuccessful, so it was leased until 1898 when it was divided into lots and auctioned. The mansion was described as *For many years in the occupation of the Everett family who at great expense added very important additions to the original mansion.* The farmhouse, farm buildings, kennels and houses were all sold.

During the First World War Greenhill House was a YMCA and convalescent home attached to the Military Hospital. It was initially occupied by British troops preparing to leave for France, but after 1916 it was taken over by the Australian Forces.

After the war, life in the house returned to normal. It was owned by Mr and Mrs Basil Hoare and renamed Sutton Veny House probably in the early 1920s.

John Frederic Everett

In 1929 the house was bought by Lady Mary Lacey. Her husband, Sir Francis, was the first man to be knighted for services to cricket (indeed the first person to be knighted in acknowledgement for services for any sport).

Jobs Mill

ONE MILE WEST of the village, beside the River Wylye beyond Southleigh Woods, is Job's Mill, the former grist mill of Sutton Veny. It derives its name from the two tenants who occupied it for most of the 18th century – father and son, both called Job Lewis. It was later leased by the Everetts, clothiers of Heytesbury, but never converted to cloth processing.

The mill building was converted to a private house and garden, making good use of the river and mill stream. The garden is open to the public on a summer Sunday each year under the National Gardens Scheme.

The Woolpack

The Village, Sutton Veny.   Nº 545.

The Woolpack 1914-18

THE WOOLPACK STANDS at a point in the village where the valley road from Wilton to Warminster crosses the Maiden Bradley to Norton Bavant road – an ideal place to build an inn. It is not known if the building shown was the first inn at this spot, nor if it was the first with this name. The Woolpack, however, does appear in the 1848 Kelly's Trade Directory. The present Woolpack was built for the Lamb Brewery, Frome in 1931.

Manymans Mead, 32-35 High Street

Manymans Mead

THIS IS BY FAR the oldest dwelling at the Newnham end of Sutton Veny. In 1265 Edith and Mabel, daughters of Hereward of Newnham, granted land in Newnham to the Priory of Maiden Bradley and it remained the landowner until it was dissolved by Henry VIII in 1536.

A few years earlier, in 1532, the main dwelling and lands belonging to the estate were leased to Thomas Hinton and his sons, with the stipulation they would, within four years, rebuild the existing house. This was to be at their own expense apart from all the great timbers for the building which would be funded by the Priory. There is evidence that this is what happened because today, the existing timber framed extension to the original stone walled building contains massive oak beams identified as of an ecclesiastical cut dating back to the medieval period.

Later, in the Longleat Lease Book 6 of May 1691, there is a record of Josias Hinton living in the farmhouse. The Hintons were a well to do farming family, a branch of which lived in the property from 1532 until at least 1800, almost 300 years. The 1886 OS map of Sutton Veny shows the farmhouse had been divided into four 4 cottages.

Manymans Mead eastern end

The eastern end cottage (the end on in this picture), was occupied by Henry and Charlotte Crouch. A relative, Jane Taylor, tells that they were a family of six boys and two girls. Edward, a middle boy, became a groom at Eastleigh Court, Bishopstrow. One day, while exercising a horse, he was thrown and sustained injuries which caused his death.

Frederick Crouch campaign medals

Walter, the eldest, was killed in 1917 at Arras, France aged 27. Recently, Jane went over to Arras with some soil from his Sutton Veny garden, and sprinkled it over his grave.

Frederick fought in the South African campaign 1899–1901 (the Boer War). He kept a diary in which he recorded the day-to-day routine and some of the fighting. He also wrote some poems, one of which is *Out upon the Veldt*.

There are two further Crouch family coincidences. Frederick saw action at Ladysmith and by chance a house owner in Sutton Veny has a garden bench on the back of which is a plaque with an inscription that tells that it was made ...*from the teak of HMS Terrible whose guns relieved Ladysmith*.

The second coincidence is that Jane had another relative who was a gunner on HMS Terrible during the bombardment.

Out upon the Veldt

1.
Out upon the Veldt dear Mother,
I am sitting in a tent.
It is my present home dear Mother,
With which I have to be content.
The water rate and rent collectors
Never trouble us with calls.
Still flies and gnats dear Mother

Buzz around as evening falls.
Farewell Mother shall I ever
Get a wash and shave again
Yes I live in hope Dear Mother
If I once reach home again.

2.

Out upon the Veldt dear Mother,
I am watching for the foe.
While the men on sentry Mother
Softly come and go.
Hark the sound of distant firing
Tis the guns of Old Doom Paul
No, alas we find it's thunder
As the rain begins to fall
Farewell Mother shall I ever
Get my clothing dry again
Yes I live in hope dear mother
If I once reach home again.

3.

Out upon the Veldt dear Mother,
I am preparing for my bed
Picking up the stones dear Mother
That I find beneath my head.
Then I lay me down to slumber
And dream of long ago
When I wake again to wonder
Have I done with Sentry go.
Farewell dear Mother shall I ever
See a feather bed again.
Yes I live in hope dear mother
If I once reach home again.

4.

Out upon the Veldt dear Mother,
I am going to break my fast.
With a piece of biscuit Mother
Though perhaps it is the last.
What you say that bread is coming

And some coffee yes it's true
But unto the milk and sugar
We have bid a fond adieu
Farewell dear Mother shall I ever
Get a good square meal again.
Yes I live in hope dear mother
If I once reach home again.

After the Second World War, an adjoining cottage was occupied by Dick and Myrle King-Smith as their first home. He went on to be a farmer and then a primary school teacher at Farmborough near Bath. He is best known for writing the book, The Sheep-Pig, which in 1995 was adapted for the film Babe.

In 1970 the four cottages were converted into a single dwelling and renamed Manymans Mead, with a nodding reference to the medieval open field system which stretched out from the back towards Longbridge Deverill.

Little Hall

T HERE HAVE BEEN two congregational chapels built on or near this site. The first was built in 1793 and the second was built on the present gravel and garage area, in 1856.

In 1818 the chapel had a school but it became too small and dilapidated, so in 1870 a larger one was built adjoining the chapel. It had space for 80 pupils and whilst most of the children were Chapel, some were Church of England and attended there because it was near their homes. The school had financial support from the British School Society which explains why it is sometimes referred to as the British School (and sometimes the Chapel School).

The school entrance was from Chapel Drain (a word derived from drangway – a narrow lane) on the east side of the building with an intriguing Normanesque doorway – reflecting the Norman style in which the chapel had been built in 1869. Records show that in

Normanesque entrance to the school

1889 there were only 40 pupils, and in 1903 this had fallen to 24. The school closed in 1910.

In addition to being a school, the room was used for social gatherings, lectures and meetings. During the Second World War, it was used as a NAAFI and afterwards it continued to be used for village meetings and as a function room for weddings and parties.

It was sold in 1970 and the schoolroom was converted into a house. With a reference to its previous historic use, the owners named it Little Hall.

Old Police House

THE VILLAGE BOBBY used to live in one of the three Greenhill estate staff houses above the Woolpack crossroads, but in 1933 this house was built to a more or less standard police design typical in other Wiltshire villages, with 'County Police' displayed on the front. When necessary, the sitting room doubled as an office and interview room.

A wind-up air raid siren and some red paraffin lamps were kept handy in the bicycle shed beside the house and standing against the roadside hedge was a black notice board with 'Wiltshire Constabulary' in white iron lettering.

During the 1960s the village policeman was withdrawn and the house became the home for a police car driver. In due course, he was able to buy it and not wanting passers-by to be misled into thinking that a helpful local copper could still be found there, he placed a large wooden sign over the words County Police with 'Wazanik' carved on it. A nice touch, but it did cause some confusion a few years later, when a family with the surname of Woznica moved into the village!

The Warminster UFO is not recorded as being seen over Sutton Veny but one resident who saw it was Constable George Russell, a traffic policemen who lived in the Police House. He recalled a sighting in the mid 1960s whilst on patrol on the A36 at Codford with a colleague:

We were patrolling at night, from recollection about 1 or 2 in the morning. We were driving along the High Street in Codford towards Warminster for our grub break. Suddenly we became aware of something to our right, it was very low in the sky. At first I thought it was a helicopter it was about that size, and looked like the glass front of one. It was a huge great dome, the surface glowing orange, like a light in the cockpit. Then I realised if the inside was illuminated the pilot would be unable to see out into the darkness! I was also aware that there was no noise. After a moment the 'Thing', moving unbelievably quickly and totally silently, sped off towards Manor Farm then off to the North East. We turned round to follow it but it disappeared from view in the direction of the Plain.

Bell House

The Bell Inn

THE BUILDING DATES from the early 17th century. Originally it was the Bell Inn and in 1841, it was recorded as being a tavern (which is the same as an inn, both offering accommodation and drink). For a while during the First World War, it was dubbed the Australia Hotel, presumably as a gesture to the troops.

Jane Major
Jane, one of eight children, was born in April 1791. Her father rented some land at Greenhill where he grew potatoes for sale at the markets in nearby towns and on one occasion when he was late home from Salisbury, she walked the 20 miles to bring him safely back.

She married her first husband Edward Hinton, in 1813. She could neither read nor write because her parents could not afford schooling, and signed the marriage certificate with her mark 'X'. Six years later Edward took the Bell Inn and Jane became the landlady. She bore nine children only losing one in infancy, rearing two daughters and six sons to adulthood.

Edward died in 1835 and three years later Jane married her second husband, Francis Major, a wool sorter. She continued to run the Inn for 28 years after his death in 1844. There is an interesting aside about her in that although beer had always been brewed at the Bell, Jane declared that she never drank it, only cider!

She retired at 71 after running the inn for 44 years, and settled into a cottage in the High Street.

Although from humble beginnings Jane succeeded in business, learnt to write – she was one of 179 parishioners who, in 1886, signed an illuminated address in gratitude for the building of St John's church.

Her obituary mentions her recollections of some significant historic events, particularly the Battle of Waterloo and the end of the Napoleonic War with memories of seeing French prisoners of war being littered down and fed at The Bell and The Anchor stables overnight in Warminster as they marched in custody from Bristol to Southampton for repatriation (a sight to be repeated several generations later with German prisoners of war in Sutton Veny).

Jane Major on her 100th birthday

In later years the Bell had a busy trade, with a full sized skittle alley at the back. The inn was owned at one time by the Lamb Brewery and in 1960 it closed down, was sold and converted into a dwelling house, and renamed Bell House[34].

The Knapp

T HERE HAVE BEEN four generations of the Ellings family living in the village. John (1720-1755) may have started the family woolstapling business at the Knapp.

The seven-storey woolstore in the yard dwarfed the house. The total floor area was five times larger than St John's. It was a prominent feature on the village skyline.

At the beginning of the First World War, not all the camps were ready for occupation when the troops arrived, and as a consequence many were billeted in tents. One night a gale blew some down and a number of

Woolstore arrowed

The Knapp

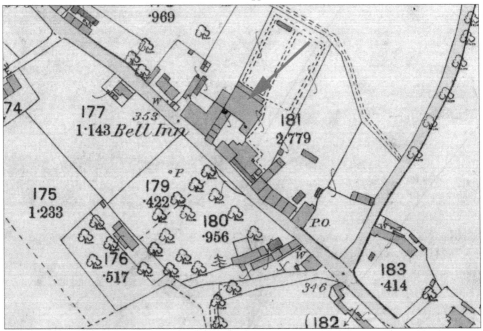

The Woolstore. OS 1886

troops were sent to the woolstore to sleep. Although, by then, the building had been empty for a long time, sheep ticks were still in the building. The soldiers became infested and next morning half naked men were seen sitting in the rain delousing themselves.[31]

DON'T WORRY!
I'm Quite Comfortable at SUTTON VENY.

Interestingly, Robert Elling's diary entry of the event is more aloof: *11 November 1914. About 200 men slept in warehouse and saddle room. 12 November. Royal Engineers complain of 'fleas' a large proportion leave tomorrow*

In time, the woolstore became unsafe, and it was pulled down in 1920. The site subsequently formed part of a sunken garden.

Robert was a successful businessman and indications of his prominence in the village can be gauged with his name appearing from time to time:

A principal signatory of the 1866 Illuminated Address commemorating the building of St John's Church. His name as a Churchwarden embossed on one of the church bells when it was re-cast in 1886. Donated the St John's eagle lectern. In the 1910 Register of Land Values, he is identified as owning most of the houses and land in the High Street, Dymocks Lane and Hill Road.[35] His prominent tombstone (the largest in the churchyard) adjacent to the south door of St Johns.

Family papers tell us something about Robert's character. He was an energetic and popular man and hunted virtually until the end of his life in 1916. In his obituary in The Field magazine, there is a touching passage: *After the funeral service was over, as we were turning away from the grave beside the church...Dick Elling his son, turned and said to the huntsman, 'We won't draw any more Charlie; we'll go home now'. Adcock blew the long notes on his horn which collects the hounds and tells everyone that the day's sport is over. May the English soil rest lightly on a fine old English gentleman.*

There is a curiosity about the field immediately opposite the house; its ground level is significantly higher than the High Street and other surrounding land. In about 1895, Robert had the soil from the land adjoining it, dug out and deposited on his field, leaving a flat piece of ground. The reason for this is not known but it would have been something significant because the cost of digging out an estimated 10,000 tonnes of earth would have been substantial. The business enterprise he had in mind at the time (he was aged 68), is not known.

The Elling Steps

Robert's son Richard (who had married a corn merchant's daughter and carried on in that trade) inherited his father's properties on his death in 1916 and sold almost everything.

The Old House

A Mr H F Baker of Salisbury wrote an account of being taken to visit Mrs Jane Major on 17 May 1889 *when she spoke of an old house, by the roadside, at the turn going to Little Sutton, which was a public house with the sign of the Cock and Dog.*

A newspaper article gives an interesting report about this house: *There used to be a coaching inn at the other end of the village where the road climbs once more to leave it. Here is a charming residence of thatch and ancient stone, called appropriately The Old House. Built at the end of the 17th century, it was once believed to be the King James the First Inn, and was the last port of call for stagecoaches going up the long climb Hill Road to Shaftesbury.*

The Old House (artist unknown)

After changing horses at the inn, the stagecoach would climb out of Sutton Veny, by a steep and narrow lane directly across the road from the inn topping the heights of Whiten Hill and crossing the lonely downs.

The Manor House

The medieval manor house became the home of the Rector in about 1590. It was known as The Rectory. This continued until 1911, when the Diocese sold it and built a new rectory at the other end of the rectory park. So, that then became The Rectory and what had been The Rectory became The Manor again. In 1986 the Diocese sold The Rectory and it became known as The Old Rectory, and they built a new rectory at the other side of the rectory park, calling it The Rectory. Until…

Sutton Veny Manor was the medieval manor house of Great Sutton and Fenny Sutton. Its early ownership is somewhat torturous but in the mid-14th century, it came under the single ownership of Sir Thomas Hungerford. It remained in his family until about 1685, when the estate was sold to Sir Stephen Fox who broke the estate in smaller parcels and sold them on. The house itself became the Parsonage.

The Manor House

As with most buildings such as this, there have been a number of alterations, adjustments and restorations over the centuries. Elsewhere in this book reference is made to the comfortable living enjoyed by Sutton Veny rectors; this is evidenced by the additional wings that were added in the middle of the 19th century by the Rector, G Powell, for his wife, seven children and five in-house staff.

In 1911 the Diocese built a new rectory in Bests Lane and as a consequence, after over 300 years it became The Manor once more.

A number of interesting people have lived in the property:

Sir William Nicholson. A significant and prominent painter producing work during the first half of the 20th century. Whilst his paintings included still-life, landscape and portraits, he is also known as a wood engraver, illustrator, author of children's books and a designer for the theatre. He also, incidentally, taught Sir Winston Churchill to paint.

His first wife died in the 1918 flu epidemic and he remarried Edith (also a professional painter, using the name Elizabeth Drury), and they moved to the Manor in 1923.

William was *an amusing man, sparkling in conversation with a quick-moving elegance wearing a spotted shirt, yellow waistcoat, high colour olive green coat, white duck trousers and cloth topped boots with mother of pearl buttons.* He was described as a light-hearted rebel, a description which reflected his and Edith's Bohemian lifestyle. They did not 'conform': they painted the building white and renamed it The White House (although there is little sign of that now), they got rid of as many of the old beams as possible and asked Lutyens to design 18th century doors to keep out the cold in their 14th century Great Hall. William designed and painted shutters to cover the draughty medieval windows, with figures from playing cards, and laid down a black and white chequered lino floor in the hall.

One of the family members recalls how *the house was alive with children and life was glorious.* There were always plenty of people about with a stream of well-known figures and personalities passing through.

Entertainment and performances would be put together with family and villagers, for the Nicholsons were persuasive and would not take 'No' for an answer. He produced a Chaucer pageant, complete with hobby horses he had designed for the occasion and also *A Midsummer Night's Dream* was also performed in the garden.

The family left the village in about 1935 and William was knighted for his services to art in 1936. He later recalled his time in Sutton Veny as his happiest years.

Snow in the Horseshoe (1927)

Nicholson's works are now on display in museums and galleries throughout the world and these two pictures are good examples of the landscapes and still lifes for which he is well known and admired. These two were painted while he lived at the White House. Both are reproduced by kind permission of Desmond Banks ©.

Mixed Flowers in a Mug (1929)

Charles and Mary Goodall. Circa 1935. Charles was a banker and employed gardeners and a chauffeur. He insisted on paying his staff with unused notes and coins because he would never use old ones. When he died in 1968, his coffin was wheeled on the bier from the house, across the park to St John's. It has not been used since.

The Old School House

T HE EARLIEST MENTION of an actual building used for education in the village was in 1850 when a school was built from two converted cottages. The deeds stipulated that the pupils should be taught, ... reading, writing, the rudiments of arithmetic. . . and that the Holy scriptures should be taught and carefully explained to

Early 1900s

all the children in the said school according to the doctrine of the Church of England.

Nine years later the *Warburton Census of Wiltshire Schools* records about the school, *...scholars, mixed, are taught by a steady young mistress who has gained a certificate. The room is tolerably good with boarded floor. Instruction and discipline are both rudimentary.*

Before the 1870 Education Act, and for some time afterwards, it was the local clergyman who very often assumed responsibility for the establishment of a village school and who helped to cover its running costs from his own income. This seems to be the case for the school at Sutton Veny but since his was one of the richest livings in the county, worth £800 a year, perhaps he could afford it! The rector was supported by the local Greenhill squire, Joseph Everett, Lord Bath, Lord Heytesbury and several other individuals. Parents who could afford to do so, paid a weekly fee of penny or tuppence.

With the 1870 Act came a growing compulsion that all children between the ages of 5 and 13 went to school. It quickly became apparent that a larger building was needed. A new school was built next to St John's Church in the High Street.

Barters Forge

T HE BARTERS WERE a long established Sutton Veny family going back, at least, to the early 18th century. They were a family of blacksmiths, wheelwrights, builders, carpenters, coffin makers, undertakers and sexton. In the 1890s two brothers, Joseph and John Barter, made the bier that is kept in St Leonard's.

Barters Forge

William Barter was awarded land by the 1804 Enclosure Award and his (probable) great grandson, Harry Barter, was killed in Northern France at Cambrai on 8 October 1918, just a month before the end of the First World War.

Set in the ground under the gravel near the archway, is the jig used to hold the wagon wheel steady whilst being fitted with its red hot wrought iron tyre.

Mulberry House

Mulberry House

THE ORIGINAL PART of Mulberry House was built in 1733 and called The Rectory Cottage. This was changed to The Cottage just before the First World War and renamed Mulberry House in 2005.

In 1949 it was let to Lt Col Francis Weldon MVO MBE MC. In 1953 he commanded the King's Troop Royal Horse Artillery in the Queen's Coronation procession. He was an outstanding horseman and an equestrian and Olympic champion. In the 1956 Stockholm Olympic Games, he won a team gold medal in eventing and received an individual bronze medal. He also became European champion in 1953, 1954 and 1955.

Huntsmans Lodge

Huntsmans Lodge

THIS WAS ONE of the houses built by Joseph Everett in about 1860 and occupied by hunt staff. The kennels and stables were next door.

At one time the house was occupied by the head gardener at Greenhill House, a Mr Wicks. On going out to check the chickens one day, Mrs Wicks fell down an uncharted well and drowned.

Greenhill Farmhouse

ORIGINALLY TWO STAFF COTTAGES were built in 1859 as part of the Everett's extensive building programme when they bought the Greenhill Estate. They were subsequently converted into a single dwelling to became the farmhouse for the 209 acre Greenhill farmland, let to the Pickford family in 1929.

The house was sold and became a private house when the estate was broken up in 1977.

Greenhill House (No. 5 Greenhill).

G REENHILL HOUSE (originally called Greenhill Farmhouse) was built in 1858 and reflected the manager's status; there are signs of a tack room, servants' accommodation and a large cellar.

The portal over the front door has the Everett's griffin emblem, similar versions of which also appear on the two lodge houses of Sutton Veny House.

In 1978 the house, stables and outbuildings were sold to the developer who three years later had built the two small adjacent housing developments.

APPENDICES

Appendix 1

Aircrew Remembrance Society

A non-political society dedicated in helping relatives of fallen & missing airmen from the 1939-45 air war. Preserving the memories, photographs and documents of those from all nations who paid the ultimate sacrifice.

THE LAST FLIGHT OF JUNKERS JU 88A-14.
23 APRIL 1944.

Mission: Bristol - England
Date: 23rd April 1944
Time: 02.00 hrs
Unit: 4 Staffel./Kampfgeschwader 30
Type: Junkers Ju 88A-14
Werke.Nr.144501
Coded: 4D + FM
Location: Manor Farm, Hill Deverill, near Warminster, Wiltshire, England.

Pilot: Unteroffizier. Rudolf Detering. 62748/137 – Captured POW. Born 17.10.1920 in Lübbecke/Westf.

Observer: Unteroffizier. Johann Agten. 62748/138 – Captured POW. Born 27.08.1920 in Gronau/Westf.

Radio/Op: Unteroffizier. Walter Kempter. 62706/4 – Captured POW. Born 12.04.1920 in Nenzing, Krs. Konstanz.

Gunner: Unteroffizier.   Helmut Trauwald. 63659/107 – Killed. Born 01.04.1923 in Gr.Rudminnen.

Aircraft. Ju 88A-14

REASON FOR LOSS:

On the morning of April 23rd 1944, Luftwaffe bomber crews of the Stabs Schwarm and three Staffeln of II and III Gruppe KG30 flew from their base at Bad Zwischenahn to the French airfield of Paris/Orly. Immediatly after landing, the mechanics and ground crews were preparing to re-fuel and re-arm the Junkers Ju 88's in preparation for the coming night's mission to England.

    At approximately 16.30 hrs that Sunday afternoon, the Gruppenkommandeur of the II Gruppe, Major Pflueger, briefed the assembled young aircrews in detail. Their target was merely described as 'The City of Bristol', the area to be attacked would be marked by a square of red & white flares, dropped by Pathfinder aircraft.

    The route laid down for the II Gruppe was to fly from Paris/Orly to Guernsey, which was the rendezvous and first turning point, then to the second turning point which was the mouth of the River Usk. The bombing run was to be made in a north - south direction, bombs to be dropped at a height of 16,000 feet, then after the attack all to return to Orly. The bomb loads that the ground crews were preparing for the raid are as follows; 2 AB 500 incendiary containers, one filled with ordinary 1-kilo I.B's having explosive noses (IBEN), with a further ten 50-kilo phosphorus incendiary bombs.

    One particular crew at the briefing listened intently to their Gruppenkommandeur, they had already flown over 20 missions and all wore the Iron Cross 1st Class and the

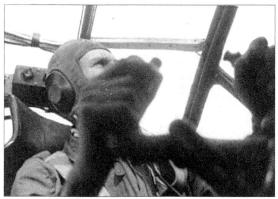

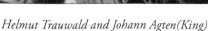

Helmut Trauwald and Johann Agten(King)

20 mission bronze war flights badge. These four young men had a close bond together, but little did they know that one of them lose their life during this coming night's operation.

Their aircraft for this mission was the 4D + FM, a Junkers Ju 88A-14, Wnr.144501. At 23.50 to 00.10 hours some 15 to 20 aircraft of II/KG30 took off from Orly between one and two minute intervals, the 4D + FM was the 7th in the group airborne.

Uffz. Detering headed on the prescribed course, flying at first at a height of between 400 - 800 metres to a point in the Caen area. From here their Ju 88 gradually gained height. Guernsey was reached at 01.15 hours, by the time they had reached landfall at a point near Weymouth, they had attained an altitude of 6,000 metres. The remainder of the crew settled in their relevant positions and focused their eyes to the night skies in search for the RAF night fighters. At no time did they see any other aircraft from the Gruppe, they were alone!

At 01.10 hours (BST) on the 24th April, a Mosquito XVII/A1, coded with the letter T for Tommy of No.125 Newfoundland Squadron prepared to take off for a night interception sortie from RAF Hurn. GCI Sopley had a fix on an incoming enemy aircraft heading on a course to the west of England.

The enthusiastic aircrew scrambled to their aircraft, in this case this was a very experienced crew, S/L Eric Barwell DFC, a veteran since 1940 with five enemy aircraft destroyed and his trusty navigator F/L David Haigh. They were ordered to orbit R sector where many searchlights were seen in the distance along the south coast, towards the west country. The lights from searchlights were seen through the low stratus cloud, they flew on towards their incoming target.

Meanwhile, Uffz. Detering and his crew had passed the south coast, radio operator **Uffz Walter Kempter** takes up the story.......

'At the south coast of England we anticipated heavy AA fire, but it was strangely quiet, we of

Uffz, Walter Kempter   *Walter pictured in flight gear*

course expected the RAF night fighters. I was on alert, yet I did not see any, neither did my
three comrades. We lost some height to about 4,000 metres and started to bundle out packets
of silver foil strips of Duppel in case we have been picked up by British radar. Suddenly
and unexpectedly I felt a heavy strike against our machine, then a searing mass of flames.
We had been hit by a night fighter! In such a terrifying situation there is, as you probably
can imagine, no time for talking. Without hesitation I un-locked the emergency exit and
immediately bailed out, having no concern of still being connected to the wireless set and
oxygen equipment. Once clear of the aircraft I counted 21 - 30 seconds before I opened my
parachute. I had to be clear of the burning plane. In which order we all left the aircraft I do
not know, but regulations state that in an emergency situation, I, the radio operator releases
the rear part of the canopy and jump, followed by the navigator, pilot and gunner.

I remember experiencing a feeling of calm as I floated in the air, it was somehow
wonderful. Above me the night sky, beneath me Great Britain wrapped in total darkness. A
new chapter in my life will now begin, an uncertain future lay before me and I was inclined
to pray. I looked above for my parachute, interrupting my thoughts and bringing me back
to reality. My parachute was partially damaged, torn in two places. I immediately became
terribly frightened, but thankfully the chute did not tear anymore. I hoped soon to land on
'mother earth'. I could not perceive the distance to the ground as there was some mist which
I guessed were about 2 - 300 metres above ground. As I floated into the mist I withdrew my
signal pistol and fired one shot towards the ground so as to try and prepare my landing. As

I fired I was instantly aware of the rebounding fireball, it was the ground and I am suddenly on British soil. I was unhurt except for a slight sprain to my left foot. My thoughts returned of my comrades, did they get out in time or have they perished!

CAPTIVITY

When my eyes had finally adapted to the darkness surrounding me, I saw nearby a dark silhouette which I believed to be an outline of a house. I approached with caution until I realised that it was in fact not a house but a stack of straw. I wondered if these stacks were a feature of this region. That night I spent in the stack, I could not sleep and nobody thankfully found me. It was about 5.00 a.m that I decided to set off not knowing which direction to take. The landscape was very hilly and divided by fences. Knowing that there was no way home I thought of what I should do. My main problem was how to become a prisoner without any danger of reprisals from the local people. I decided to find the nearest village and give myself up to the local police. Before I left I hide all my personal belongings in the stack, my parachute and a large amount of French money, which I planned to spend in Paris after our return from the raid. I hoped that maybe I could find some of my comrades or even our plane, but this was not to be.

From time to time I took out my English pocket dictionary and learnt my first few words of essential English. At about 12 noon I finally came across a village. I carefully approached the first house and knocked on the door, someone answered, 'come in', I then opened the door into the kitchen where an elderly lady stood washing in a bowl, she was alone and showed no fear when confronted by a German airman. In my broken English I asked her for a telephone, but I could not understand her reply, again I stammered 'have you a telephone, police, police'. This she must have understood and took me outside and pointed to a house across the road. I crossed the road and entered the half opened door, there was a telephone, I hesitated momentarily, then I felt someone's hand on my shoulder. It was an elderly man, he must have seen me going into the house and became suspicious and followed me in. As we faced each other I said, I am German, he then gestured me to wait while he made a telephone call, his eyes never left me for a minute. He then took me outside and we walked to the policeman's house but he was not there so we waited. Nearby to us there were four or five women, they showed me no hostility, on the contrary, when I made a gesture for a drink each one of these kind women gave me a glass of water which I appreciated very much.

Half an hour passed then a car arrived, a policeman and a civilian got out and approached me, the latter addressed me in perfect German. I told him my story but had expected to be overpowered by force because I still had my pistol with me. However, when I attempted to climb into the car, the policeman threw his arm around my neck and disarmed me. I made no resistance only resignation. I held up my hands and said; 'Ich bin Ihr gefangener' (I am your prisoner).

The two men took me by car to Warminster, where they delivered their prisoner to the police station. A short while after a civilian entered the room and spoke to me in perfect German. He asked me many questions and asked me if I was injured, I replied I am well except for slight pains in my left foot, which he in turn answered: then you can consider yourself more lucky than your comrades! I asked him what he knew of my friends? He said that they had found our gunner Helmut dead with bullet wounds attributed to the night fighter attack. The other two had broken bones and that our observer will probably never be able to walk again. Was this true, I did not know. After my first interrogation at the police station I was given a hot cup of coffee and some cake. I was then taken to my cell where I could get some sleep. Later three soldiers arrived at my door armed to the teeth and escorted me to the train station by jeep. Around midnight we reached a station in London, then began eight weeks of interrogation, not very agreeable, but that's another story............'

*Former NFS Fireman John House points to where
he found the body of Helmut Trauwald*

The remains of Uffz. Kempter's aircraft broke up in the air over Manor Farm, Hill Deverill, a small village south of Warminster, Wiltshire. The wreck of the Ju 88 was completely burnt out after exploding in the air close to Manor Farm. Firefighters from the Warminster NFS did an excellent job in quelling a serious outbreak of fire caused by falling phosphorous bombs on a farm occupied by Captain Booth. Manor Farm had

FRIDAY. APRIL 28TH 1944.

Three Nazi Airmen Captured

Escaped from Blazing Plane in the South Country

Three of the crew of a German plane brought down near a village in the South West during a raid early on Monday morning were captured the same day. One was found dead nearby by a member of the N.F.S. (Fireman J. House). The plane was one of five shot down when enemy raiders switched their attack to the South and Southwest coasts, although the enemy radio gave the announcement that the object of attack was Bristol.

The first of three Germans surrendered to Major Fane when he awoke the household at three o'clock in the morning. He was bleeding profusely from wounds and his injuries included a broken arm. Three miles away another surrendered to Mr. Philip Burt, a Home Guardsman. That there was something amiss was notified by a spaniel dog barking frantically and when Mr. Burt made investigations he found the wounded airman lying beside his parachute. He had injuries to his foot.

The third of the three who escaped was found near Mr. Pinniger's farm. He was more fortunate than his comrades having escaped injury in his hurried descent from the burning plane.

Meanwhile the N.F.S. were doing excellent work in quelling an outbreak of fire caused by falling phospherous bombs on a farm occupied by Capt. Booth. A house in the village had a miraculous escape, the plane passing over within a few feet and crashed nearby. A 70-ton straw rick was completely "gutted," having been destroyed in about half an hour. The plane itself was a burning furnace but this was controlled by means of a mobile dam using foam.

It was indeed fortunate that the village was spared the horror of total destruction which might easily have happened had the plane fallen in the midst of the houses.

A warning not to tamper with bombs or any other object found on the ground after an air raid has been made in an announcement made by the Ministry of Home Security.

Occupiers of land should report at once the finding of small fire-bombs or of suspicious holes to a Warden or the police. Reporting the find of bombs is a legal obligation and it is an offence not to report.

The public are also asked to warn the children not to tamper or handle ammunition which might be found after a crash as it is an extremely dangerous practice.

The Warminster Journal report 28 April 1944

a miraculous escape, the plane passing low overhead and crashing in fields adjacent to the farm. A 70 ton straw rick was completely gutted having been destroyed in less than half an hour. The remains of the Ju 88 was a burning furnace but the NFS controlled this by means of using a mobile dam using foam. It was indeed fortunate that the village was spared the horror of complete destruction which might easily have happened had the plane fell in the midst of the houses. A warning was issued not to tamper with the bombs or any other object found on the ground after the crash.

As for the remaining crew members, the pilot, Uffz Detering gave himself up to Major Fane when he awoke the household at 3.00 a.m in the morning. He was bleeding profusely from his wounds, plus he was nursing a broken arm. Three miles away, the observer Uffz Agten surrendered to Home Guardsman Mr Philip Burt. Mr Burt found the wounded airmen lying beside his parachute after being alerted by the barking of a dog. The two airmen were admitted to hospital for the treatment of injuries sustained. Eventually they followed the same path of interrogations that Uffz Kempter took.

In 1992 Mike Croft and Melvin Brownless flew to Stuttgart and then drove to Stockach to meet with Walter Kempter at his home. This for us was our first trip to Germany and the very first time on the Autobahn! We were really impressed with German driving skills, especially as most Autobahn's are only two laned each side. Drivers who were in the outside lane automatically pulled into the nearside lane when a faster car was approaching from behind, we thought, 'This would not happen in England'.

We arrived safely at Walter's house in the early afternoon, had a quick coffee and then we were out on a tour of the wonderful town of Stockach, which is next to Lake Constance, a truly beautiful area. After a lot of walking we returned home for dinner. Walter and his wife Lore were truly great hosts, they kindly put us up for a few days, fed us and were thoroughly charming. Unfortunately Walter passed away a number of years ago and this page of remembrance is dedicated to him and his fellow comrades, RIP.

Researched and compiled by Melvin Brownless & Mike Croft (1992) With special thanks to Walter & Lore Kempter. [36]

Appendix 2

THE NAMES OF THE SERVICEMEN INSCRIBED ON SUTTON VENY WAR MEMORIAL

FIRST WORLD WAR

George N Cooper 27 December 1917
Pte SLI
12th Bn Somerset Light Infantry. Jerusalem Memorial Panel 17
Son of George and Annie Cooper, 88 High Street, Sutton Veny. Husband of Amy Lindsay (formerly Cooper) of Park Rd, Cabramatta, Sydney, Australia

Harold C Cooper 9 September 1915
LC Cpl 9th ES
9th Bn East Surrey Regiment. Loos Memorial Panel 65-67
Son of George and Annie Cooper, 83 High St, Sutton Veny

Harry Barter 8 October 1918
Pte RMLI
1st Battalion Royal Marine Light Infantry. Missing, later reported killed in action. Commemorated in Proville Cemetery, France
Husband of Winfred A Barter, New Road, Bromham, Chippenham.

Walter Crouch 11 April 1917
Pte 2nd Wilts
2nd Bn The Wiltshire Regiment Warlincourt Halte British Cemetery Saulty, France
Son of Henry Crouch 35 High Street, Sutton Veny

F Stanley Doughty 23 May 1915
Tpr KEH
Served as a Trooper in 2nd Bn King Edwards Horse. Browns Road Military Cemetery, France

Husband of Ethel Florence Doughty, 26 Bishopstrow, Warminster

Sidney C Everett 20 December 1917
Pte 3rd Wilts
Panel 119 - 120 Tyne Cot War Memorial, Belgium

Reginald A Haines 20 September 1918
Gnr RGA
199th Siege Battery Royal Artillery. Thilloy Road Cemetery, Beaulencourt, France
Son of Joseph and Lydia Haines, 71 St Lukes Road, Totterdown, Bristol

Ernest J Hibberd 9 April 1916
Pte 5th Wilts
Panel 30 and 64 Basra Memorial. Died during the seige of Kut Al Amara, Iraq. The
8,000 British Indian Garrison was under siege by the Ottoman Army from 7 Dec 1915
- 29 Apr 16.

Hector T S Hicks 21 March 1918
Pte 2nd LRF
Served in the 2nd Bn London Regiment Royal Fusiliers. Killed in France. Pozieres
Memorial Panels 19-2, France
Son of Thomas and Annie Hicks

Sidney A Hinton 22 September 1914
Br RMA
Bombardier in the Royal Marine Artillery. In HMS Aboukir in the North Sea when it
was torpedoed and sunk by a German submarine U - 9 . Portsmouth Naval Memorial
Panel 5
Son of John and Caroline Hinton, 41 High Street, Sutton Veny.

Herbert H Hooker 8 March 1917
AB RN
Died of illness (unknown) whilst serving in HMS Victory. Haslar Royal Navy Cemetery
E26.22
Son of Leonard Hooker, 12 Deverill Road, Sutton Veny

Arthur C Pond 10 August 1918
TG AIF
An Australian serving with 11Bn AIF. Panel 63, Villers-Brettonneaux Cemetery, France
Born at Sutton Parva but enlisted at Narrogin, West Australia. Son of William and

Maria Pond of Middle Farm, Codford St Mary.

Frank Snelgrove 21 July 1917
Pte RAMC
Served in the Royal Army Medical Corps in the Advanced MT Workshops. Died in Baghdad. Named in Baghdad (North Gate) War Cemetery XV A5
Son of Charles and Maria Snelgrove, 12 Alma St, Trowbridge. Born in Sutton Veny.

Thomas Webb 24 April 17
Tpr Wilts Yeo
2nd Bn Wiltshire Regiment. Bay 7, Arras Memorial, France

Robert A Colvin 10 March 1915
Cpt & Ajt W Yorks Adjutant 2nd Battalion, West Yorkshire Regiment. Guards Cemetery, Windy Corner, Cuinchy, France
Son of James and Alice Colvin, Sutton Veny

SECOND WORLD WAR

Frank I Haskell 18 February 1944
Ldg Str RN
Leading Stoker in HMS Penelope.
Torpedoed by German Submarine U-410 near Naples. A torpedo struck her in the after engine room and was followed sixteen minutes later by another torpedo that hit in the after boiler room, causing her immediate sinking.
Son of Harry Frederick and Louisa Haskell

John B Hinton 29 May 1941
Chf Pty QFR RN
In HMS Hereward near Crete when it was sunk by German Stuka dive-bombers.
Son of Freddie and Ellen Hinton.
Husband of Annie Hinton of Calne

Peter G Hobbs 27May 1942
Major RHA
Major Acting Lt Col RHA (Bde Maj) HQ 7 Armd Bde.
Name is on the Alamein Memorial.
Brother of Paul Hobbs below.
Son of Brigadier General Reginald Frances Arthur Hobbs CB CMG DSO and of

Frances Graham Hobbs (nee Stirling) of Little Newnham, Sutton Veny.
Husband of Sylvia Hobbs.

W Paul Hobbs 12 May 1943
Lt Colonel RA
Enfidaville War Cemetery, Tunisia.
Brother of Peter Hobbs above.
Son of Brigadier General Reginald Frances Arthur Hobbs CB CMG DSO and of
Frances Graham Hobbs (nee Stirling) of Little Newnham, Sutton Veny.

Cyril E Hudd 25 October 1942
Pte QRR
1/7th Bn Queens Royal West Sussex Regiment.
El Alamein War Cemetery
Son of Frank and Lily Elizabeth M Hudd.

Ivan W Mitchell 22 October 1944
LC Bdr RA
166 bty, 56 HAA Regiment, Royal Artillery.
Madras (St Mary's) Cemetery, Chennai, India
Husband of Dorothy Mitchell, Warminster.

Hubert S Pickford 2 November 1942
RW Yeo
Sergeant Royal Wiltshire Yeomanry.
El Alamein War Cemetery
Son of George and Mabel Pickford. Sutton Veny

ENDNOTES

Reference to WSA means Wiltshire and Swindon Archives.

1   *The Place-Names of England: Wiltshire*). Gover
2   Lawsuit WSA 828/31
3   *Looking Back.* Gertrude McCracken
4   *Cal. Pat.* 1216–25, 262.
5   *Heraldry for the Local Historian and Genealogist.* Stephen Friar.
6   Tim Tatton-Brown consultant archaeologist and architectural historian.
7   Research by June Barkhouse parishioner of St Thomas's.
8   Dr Ellie Pridgeon, Leicester University 2016.
9   WSA 941/35
10 history.wiltshire.gov.uk/community accessed 22 Apr 16
11 WSA 2351/15
12 WSA 1965/5
13 John Platt *The Church of St John the Evangelist Sutton Veny* 1993.
14 *Warminster Herald.* 2 June 1866
15 WSA 1965/5
16 British Organ Archive, Birmingham)
17 Desch, R., 1970 *A short History of St John the Evangelist and the Parish of Sutton Veny. Warminster.* Private publication.
18 St John the Evangelist, Sutton Veny, Burial Registers. April 1864 to April 1919.
19 Sutton Veny Congregational Church Book 1818 to 1876. WSA 1951/1 and 2
20 https://history.wiltshire.gov.uk/community/getcensus.php?item=sutton%20veny: Accessed 15 May 2017
21 Wiltshire Family History Society Baptisms and Burials
22 https://history.wiltshire.gov.uk/community accessed 23 Jan 2017
23 https://history.wiltshire.gov.uk/community accessed 23 Jan 2017
24 Parish Housing Needs Survey Sutton Veny 2014. Wiltshire Council
25 WSA 949/11and 12
26 *Looking Back On Seventy Years Of Sutton Veny,* Gertrude McCracken. Private publication June 1981.
27 *The Inns and Taverns of Warminster.* Reg Cundick. Warminster Historical Society 1987
28 WSA 963
29 With a general acknowledgement to:
    • *Wiltshire and The Great War* by TS Crawford and,
    • *Wylye Valley 1914 Commemorative Guide and Programme* by William Mahon and,
    • Sedgwick, Cathy and Prime, Marilyn. (2015). Wiltshire OPC Project, retrieved 30 November 2015 from http://www.wiltshire- pc.org.uk/genealogy/index.php/ parish-directory/item/88-sutton-veny

30 *Tyneside Irish: 24th, 25th, 26th and 27th Service Battalions of Northumberland Fusiliers.* John Sheen.

31 *Looking Back On Seventy Years Of Sutton Veny,* Gertrude McCracken. Private publication June 1981

32 http://www.aircrewremembrancesociety.co.uk. Accessed 12 March 2017

33 Prof. Bruce Scates Montash University Australia, The Australian War Memorial (Roll of Honour, First World War Embarkation Roll) and Australian National Archives.

34 WSA 2499/350/37

35 WSA L8/1/129

ANCIENT HISTORY GLOSSARY AND SOURCES OF INFORMATION

PREHISTORY

Glossary

Cropmarks – caused by the variation in growth of crops over different types of underground structures such as ditches and walls.

Field system – a group or complex of fields which appear to form a coherent whole

Henge – a Neolithic monument consisting of a circular area delineated by a ditch with a bank outside

Hillfort – hilltop enclosure performing a variety of functions eg. meeting place/market, settlement, grain storage, defence

Long barrow – a Neolithic chambered tomb covered by a mound of earth

Pit – man-made feature with various purposes such as storage (eg. of grain), rubbish dump, extraction (eg. of clay).

Pygmy cup – a small subsidiary vessel found with burials in Bronze Age barrows. Their function is unknown but some have holes in their sides so they are sometimes called incense vessels.

Round barrow – a mound, usually covering a burial(s), surrounded by a ditch and usually of Bronze Age date. Round barrows can be classified by their form; most are **bowl barrows** (the mound is surrounded by a ditch with no intervening berm); less common are **bell barrows** (the mound and ditch are separated from each other by a berm) and **disc barrows** (the mound is small and separated from a ditch of much greater diameter by a wide berm). (Berm = area of level ground between the barrow mound and the surrounding ditch.)

Sources of information

The information about prehistoric features in Sutton Veny presented in this chapter is from two main sources: Wiltshire & Swindon Historic Environment Record (HER) maintained by Wiltshire Council www.wiltshire.gov.uk/wsher.htm The staff of the County Archaeology Service are gratefully acknowledged for their help.

The National Monuments Record (NMR) maintained by English Heritage www.pastscape.org.uk

In addition, information about the prehistoric artefacts that have been found in Sutton Veny comes from Wiltshire Museum in Devizes (www.wiltshiremuseum.org.uk) and The Salisbury Museum in Salisbury (www.salisburymuseum.org.uk) and staff at both museums are gratefully acknowledged for their assistance.

Also acknowledged are several sources of information on the Neolithic, Bronze Age and Iron Age periods in Britain and specifically in the Wylye Valley:

Prehistoric Wiltshire: an illustrated guide by Bob Clarke, 2011.

Lecture course Archaeology of the Wylye Valley given by Mark Corney, University of Bristol, 2003 – notes made by the authors.

Neolithic of the Wylye Valley 1:Millennium Re-investigation of the Corton Long Barrow, paper by Michael J. Allen and Julie Gardiner, 2001 revised 2003.

Grim's Ditch in the Landscape: a study of a linear earthwork in south Wiltshire by Sally M. Thomson, 2007. Dissertation submitted for the Postgraduate Certificate in Landscape Archaeology, University of Leicester.

Ancient Trackways of Wessex by H W Timperley and Edith Brill, 2005 edition, Nonsuch Publishing Ltd.

ROMAN

Glossary

Tessellated - this refers to a mosaic floor, where very small squares of coloured clay, (tesserae), were arranged and fixed into patterns or pictorial images to decorate the floors of villas.

Lynchets -a terraced field, usually found on a hillside, consisting of a flat strip of land, called a tread, with a steep, scarped edge (the lynchet) above and below it, which was the riser. Small, short clusters of lynchets are usually ancient, Iron Age or Roman. Longer, more extensive ones are medieval.

Sources of Information

Information on Roman features in and around Sutton Veny comes from:

Wiltshire & Swindon Historic Environment Record (HER)

The National Monuments Record (NMR)

Richard Henry Finds Liaison Officer, Salisbury Museum

Corney, Mark   Spring 2005.   The Romans in the Wylye valley.   Series of Bristol University extra-mural lectures.

Ellis, Peter, ed.   2001 *Roman Wiltshire and After.* Devizes: WANHS

Hoare, Richard Colt *Ancient Wiltshire*, volumes 1 & 2.

Howell, Danny , ed. 1989   *Warminster & District Archive*, No.3 Summer 1989. (priv.pub.)

Margary, I.   1967 *Roman Roads in Britain*.   London: John Baker.

Papworth, M.   2011 *The Search for the Durotriges*. The History Press.

SAXON

Glossary

Wiltshire Civil Pleas. The Eyre for the common plea was a royal court held by the King's justices in the country at intervals of several years and usually as part of a country wide visitation

Sources of Information

Landscape, Settlement and Society in Roman and Early Medieval Wiltshire, by Simon Draper. BAR
    British Series 419, 2006.
Warminster & District Archive, No.3 1989. Editor, Danny Howell.
Victoria County History of Wiltshire, vol.VIII, pp 61-74. Editor, E.Crittall, 1965.
Alfred's Defeat of the Vikings, by John Peddie & Patrick Dillon. The Ethandun Memorial Trust.
The Anglo-Saxon Chronicle, edited by G.Garmonsway. Dent, 1982.
Asser's Life of King Alfred, edited by S.Keynes & M.Lapidge. Penguin Books, 1983.

MEDIEVAL

Glossary

The **hide**, often encountered in old documents and especially in the Domesday Survey, was not
    a precise measurement of land. It depended on geography and the type of soil in question.
    But on average, **one hide** was the equivalent of about **120 acres**. It was the amount of land
    an eight-oxen team could plough in an agricultural year. It was also sometimes termed a
    carucate.

One **furlong** was 220 yards.
One **league** was 3 miles.
A **virgate**, later also known as a **yardland**, was usually about 30 acres.

Sources of Information

Chapman, C. 1996 *How Heavy, How Much and How Long?* Dursley: Lochin Publishing.
Crittall, E. 1965 *Victoria History of Wiltshire;* vol.viii, pp61-74. London: Institute of Historical
    Research.
Gover, J., Mawer, A. & Stenton, F., eds. 1939 *The Place-Names of Wiltshire.*Cambridge:
    University Press.
Jones, W., ed. 1865 *Domesday for Wiltshire.* London: Longman.
Keynes, S. & Lapidge, M., eds. 1983 *Alfred the Great: Asser's Life of King Alfred and other
    contemporary sources.* Middlesex: Penguin.
Thorn, C. & F., eds. 1979 *Wiltshire Domesday.* Chichester: Philimore.
Wood, M. 1981 *In Search of the Dark Ages.* London: Book Club Associates.
Phillipps' Institutions (MS) Wiltshire & Swindon Family History Centre.
Crowley, D., ed. 1989 *The Wiltshire Tax List of 1332* Trowbridge: Wiltshire Record Society,
    vol.45.
Meekings, C., ed. 1961 *Crown Pleas of the Wiltshire Eyre.* Devizes: Wiltshire Record Society,
    vol.16

INDEX

Lightning Source UK Ltd.
Milton Keynes UK
UKOW07f0224101117
312508UK00003B/19/P